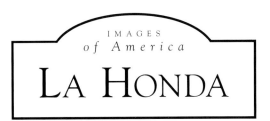

IMAGES
of America

LA HONDA

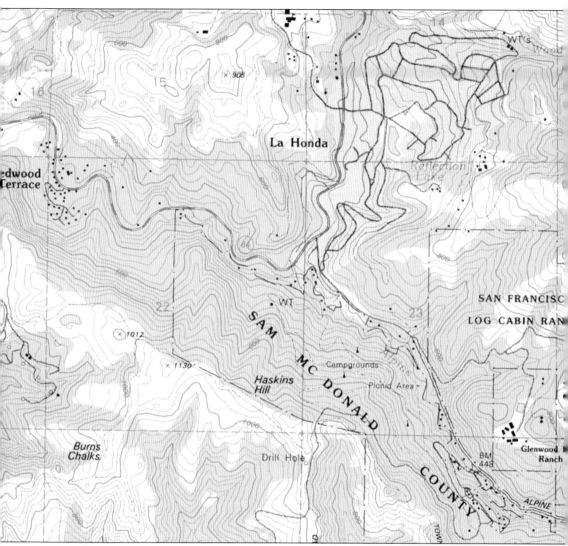

LA HONDA. A rural community in the California Santa Cruz Mountains, La Honda is located 13 miles southwest of Woodside and 14 miles northeast of Pescadero. San Gregorio is a smaller historic town 8 miles west of La Honda, where Spanish explorer Gaspar de Portola camped in 1769. Redwood Terrace and the area just south of the town of La Honda, traditionally called the Alpine, are also considered part of La Honda. (Courtesy U.S. Geological Survey.)

ON THE COVER. This 1898 photograph by Jervie Eastman shows "big wheels," one of several ways that logs were moved at the beginning of the 20th century. After the branches were removed and the logs were cut into manageable lengths, they were often dragged by oxen over greased branches called "skid rows." Once on a road, big wheels pulled by horses was much faster than using oxen. Unlike a wagon, big wheels carried the logs by chains under the axle, and some could carry logs up to 100 feet in length. (Courtesy Rob and Kathy [Zanone] Wolf.)

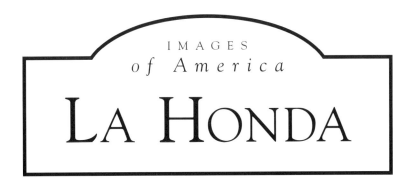

IMAGES
of America

LA HONDA

Bob Dougherty

ARCADIA
PUBLISHING

Published by Arcadia Publishing
Charleston SC, Chicago IL, Portsmouth NH, San Francisco CA

Printed in the United States of America

Library of Congress Catalog Card Number: 2006939746

For all general information contact Arcadia Publishing at:
Telephone 843-853-2070
Fax 843-853-0044
E-mail sales@arcadiapublishing.com
For customer service and orders:
Toll-Free 1-888-313-2665

Visit us on the Internet at www.arcadiapublishing.com

*This book is dedicated to Bud Foss, historian and friend,
who wrote the first history of La Honda in 1941.*

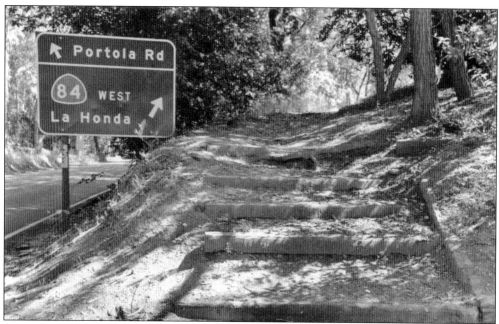

Robert Stone wrote in the June 14, 2004, issue of *New Yorker* magazine that "La Honda was a strange place, a spot on the road that descended from the western slope of the Santa Cruz Mountains toward the artichoke fields on the coast. Situated mostly within the redwood forest, it had the quality of a raw Northwestern logging town, transported to suburban San Francisco. In spirit, it was a world away from the woodsy gentility of the other Peninsula towns nearby." (Courtesy Brook Tankle.)

CONTENTS

ACKNOWLEDGMENTS

This book is the result of an outpouring of support from the whole La Honda community. The descendants of early pioneer families and other community members unselfishly shared their personal photographs, letters, and stories. I could not have weaved a historical narrative or completed this project without all their help.

I want to specifically thank Rob and Kathy (Zanone) Wolf (the last Miss La Honda Days queen) for their generosity with photographs, especially the Zanone family album; Milton Cavalli for sharing his photographs and stories of early La Honda; Hayden Coggins and Kareen Lindstrom for sharing their photographs and providing a tour of Old La Honda and Bellvale; George and Mary Bordi for their photographs, showing me the Alpine side of La Honda, and introducing me to Bud Foss; Charlie Catania for sharing some unique postcards and photographs and for giving me a copy of Bud Foss's *History of La Honda*; and of course Bud Foss, who inspired me to undertake this project.

I want to thank other community members who were also instrumental in providing important information about the area: Rick and Kit Paden for history and photographs about Troutmere and Redwood Terrace; Pam McReynolds for the photographs of the Weeks family, Sam McDonald, and others; Brook Tankle for her photographs and for introducing me to Milton Cavalli; Susan Friedman for use of her photographs that were in Charles Jones's book, *A Separate Place;* Kim and Turk Borick for photographs and information about town; Postmaster Karen Delee and Greg Baurmann at the La Honda post office for providing Pete Towne's and Billy Prior's memoirs and other leads; Jim Adams for photographs and an insider's view of the town; Lisa Law for her action photograph of Ken Kesey on Furthur; Terry and Eva Adams for the Kesey story and a tour of Kesey's former cabin; Henry Diltz for the memorable and difficult to find photograph of Neil Young; and Lin Daniels and Angela Schmidt from the La Honda House Café for photographs and for supporting historical lectures there.

In addition, the following people provided me or helped me find information to fill in many of the gaps in this project: Carol Peterson, archivist for the San Mateo County Historical Association; Matthew Dougherty for his research; Paul Fourt; June Morrall; Janet Clark; Lynette Joy Ben-Sushan Vega; Karen Shaff; John Bachelor; John Edmonds; Molly Spore-Alhadef; Michael Williams; Zane Kesey; Wavy Gravy; Chris Knorr; Angie Quinn; Carol Cipriano; Ray Roberts; Ruth Waldhauer; Gary and Nancy Woodhams; Pat and Carol Williams; Nicki Sinclair; David Strohm; and Lauren LaFauci for her invaluable last-minute reviewing.

I would also like to thank John Poultney, my editor at Arcadia Publishing, for his patience and professionalism over the length of this project.

And finally, I want to thank my family—Dan, Dianne, Dennis, and my mom—as well as the rest of my family: Jennifer and Lorenzo, Jessica, and Carolyn Douglas, for their support, understanding, and love while I disappeared over the past several months.

INTRODUCTION

La Honda is a community located in the middle of the Santa Cruz Mountains, 13 miles southwest of Woodside and 14 miles northeast of Pescadero. The scope of this book will include Old La Honda, located about three-fourths of a mile west of present-day La Honda at the fork of the La Honda and San Gregorio Creeks; Bellvale, a former small town four miles west of La Honda; and some of the Alpine area of La Honda, which is located south of the town of La Honda. This narrative and photographic history will concentrate on the early settlers of the area.

There has been much speculation about the origin of the name La Honda. One suggestion is that *La Honda* was a corruption of the Spanish words *el hondo*, which means "the deep," perhaps implying a deep canyon. A second theory is that the name comes from the word *honda*, which means "sling" in Spanish, because the early stagecoaches made a loop, or slung, around the towns of La Honda, San Gregorio, and Pescadero. Another account claims that La Honda's founder, John Sears, just called it "Honda" and the U.S. Postal Service later added "La" onto the name. Perhaps the most likely explanation is that "La Honda" is a corruption of the Spanish words *Arroyo Hondo*, meaning "deep hollow," which the area was called in the 1830s. The name was corrupted from Arroyo Hondo to Arroyo Honda by 1857 and then further corrupted to La Honda by John Sears by 1877.

For many years, a sign at the entrance to La Honda proclaimed that the population of the town was 500, although this was always a rough estimate. Today the population is over twice that number. Census data shows that the population climbed from 50 individuals in 1880 to 100 in 1910, to 500 in 1950, to 900 in 1960, and fell to 850 in 1990. Unlike the cities over the hill in Silicon Valley, the population of La Honda has not experienced rapid growth since World War II. A couple reasons for this relative stability are the inadequate water supply and strict septic regulations in the area, but another important reason is that only a certain breed of hardy people is willing to accept the problems that exist in the mountains. Residents must drive long distances to purchase food and other supplies, the winding roads are nauseating for many, night driving can be treacherous because of animals on the road, and winter storms often sever electrical and phone service. Some city dwellers may fear the spiders or mountain lions, while others may fear living beneath the towering redwoods and Douglas firs. There is no cell phone service and no gas station in La Honda. The town dramatically changes between seasons, from hundreds of motorcycles converging at Applejack's Saloon during warm summer weekends to a quiet isolation during the winter.

For the residents of La Honda, these problems are a small price to pay for what they consider the most beautiful place in the world—a world apart from nearby Silicon Valley and San Francisco. It is a place surrounded by majestic redwoods, just miles from the Pacific Ocean. Early in La Honda's history, the community was predicted to flourish. In 1916, author Phillip Alexander said in *The History of San Mateo County from the Earliest Times* that "La Honda, a beautiful mountain retreat, promises to become a second Hillsborough." Alexander describes Hillsborough as "the 'municipality of millionaires,' and richer per capita than any other city in the world. . . . With its famous Burlingame Country Club, San Mateo Polo Clubs, golf links, sweeping lawns and gardens, beautiful homes and winding drives . . . one of the show spots of the state." But Alexander's prediction proved untrue, and the residents of La Honda seem content to maintain this stasis.

Early La Honda can be seen as a microcosm of the mythologized Wild West. The early pioneers had to contend with grizzly bears, outlaws, and scarce supplies. And the local indigenous people, the Ohlone Indians, had to contend with the sudden influx of these pioneers logging the redwoods, killing the game, and taking the land. But there were no Native American uprisings, just a quiet end to the Ohlone way of life.

Only about 1,500 Ohlone Indians lived in San Mateo County when Spanish explorer Gaspar de Portola arrived in 1769. Their numbers and lifestyle scarcely affected the environment. The subsequent settlers, especially loggers, had a dramatic impact on the land and animal life, as the redwood forests were depleted of trees, and wildlife habitats were destroyed. After the prime logging days ended, La Honda became a popular tourist spot for urbanites to hunt, fish, and camp. After the Golden Gate and San Francisco–Oakland Bay Bridges were built, however, vacation destinations like Lake Tahoe and the Russian River in Sonoma County became more accessible, and La Honda's popularity waned.

Starting in the 1970s, a strong environmental movement was underway to preserve the remaining coastal and open spaces in the Santa Cruz Mountains. Because of these efforts, La Honda today is surrounded by a variety of state and local parks and open-space preserves. The land has been forgiving, and the area has been able to recover much of its original natural beauty from the logging scars from over a hundred years ago. Today none of the lumber mills exist, and all of the grand hotels near town have burned or have been torn down.

This book provides a popular account of the history of La Honda, not a deep or comprehensive account. Some important information and interesting stories have been left out or greatly summarized. Other stories have been obtained from a single source and sometimes information from multiple sources has been conflicting. But historical accuracy has been attempted, and for every story presented, there are certainly two others more interesting that were never recorded. So keep in mind the aphorism of former La Honda resident Ken Kesey when he said, "It's true even if it didn't happen."

One

NATURAL HISTORY AND THE OHLONES

Although the geologic process that created the area around La Honda has been at work for millions of years, much of the current landscape was created 2,500 to 10,000 years ago during the Pleistocene Epoch. The La Honda area is still geologically active, constantly being reshaped by water, landslides, and earthquakes.

The arrival of the Ohlone Indians predated the first Europeans by at least 3,000 years. About 40 Ohlone communities are known to have lived between San Francisco Bay and Point Sur. The Ohlone Indians around La Honda were hunter-gatherers; they managed to live relatively well without farming or herding flocks. The Ohlones were loose-knit communities associated with other Ohlone communities by bonds of trade and marriage. The Ohlones seemed to have lived in relative peace and stability before the arrival of the Europeans, although their average life expectancy was only about 40 years.

The environment of the San Francisco Bay Area has changed drastically in the last 200 years. Widespread logging for lumber, tanning bark, and firewood has altered the forests. Non-native plants have seized the meadows and hillsides. The first European settlers found the forest animals relatively unafraid of people. Stories were told that geese and ducks were so thick that several were frequently killed with each shot. The sky was filled with bald eagles, condors, and ospreys; the water was filled with salmon and trout; and the land was filled with grizzly bears, elks, antelopes, wolves, and mountain lions.

It is impossible to completely reconstruct the world around La Honda when the Ohlones were the only people in the area because they did not record their observations. Many animal species disappeared through hunting and habitat destruction without much notice, except perhaps the grizzly bears. Grizzlies feared nothing and killed livestock and occasionally settlers in the area until the late 1800s. The hunting and killing of the last grizzlies were often recorded as a testament to civilizing the West.

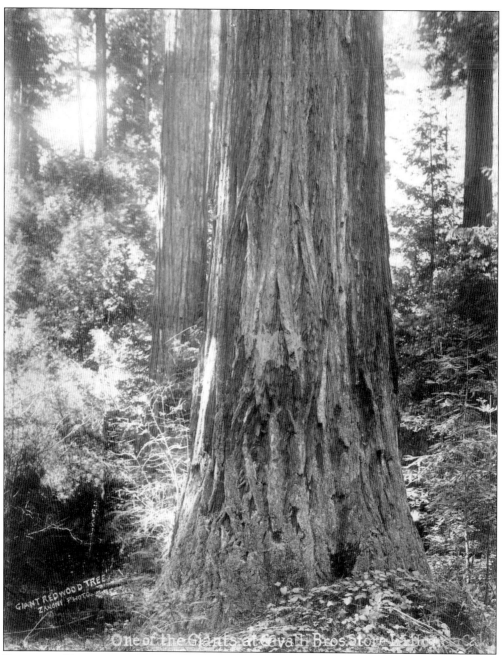

REDWOODS (*SEQUOIA SEMPERVIRENS*), 1940. Most of the old growth redwood trees have been logged in the La Honda area and replaced by second-growth redwoods and other trees. Many redwoods were over 1,000 years old and over 30 feet in circumference before they were logged. Not only are individual redwood trees ancient by human standards, but the redwood species has not changed since before the time of dinosaurs. Redwoods are the tallest trees in the world, and Douglas firs, also common in the La Honda area, are the second tallest trees. The Ohlone people in the area considered the redwood trees sacred. (Courtesy Charlie Catania.)

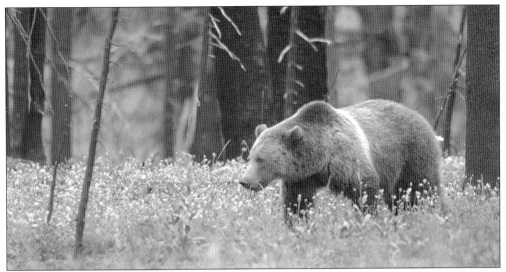

GRIZZLY BEARS (*URSUS ARCTOS HORRIBILIS*). Grizzlies devoured livestock and were a serious threat to the natives and early settlers of La Honda. In the mid-1800s, a man named Ryder, who was looking for his lost oxen, walked toward a rustling in the bushes before realizing his mistake —it was a mother grizzly with cubs. The bear stood up and grabbed Ryder, but he managed to stab the bear and then play dead. But before the bear left, she gave a final blow that took off Ryder's ear and half of his face. "Grizzly" Ryder awoke to his face being stitched up with needle and thread to stop the bleeding. That is the origin of the name Bear Gulch Road near town. Dick Bartley was said to have killed the last grizzly bear near La Honda in the late 1880s. (Courtesy U.S. Forest Service.)

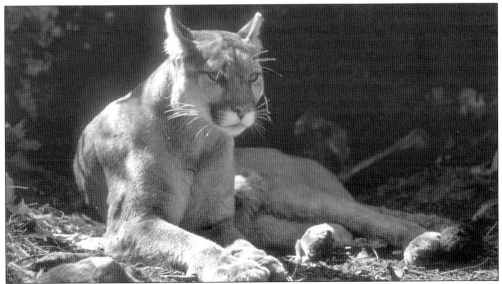

MOUNTAIN LIONS (*FELIS CONCOLOR*). The mountain lion is a large solitary cat whose primary food is deer. It lives throughout the Santa Cruz Mountains, including La Honda, but is shy and rarely seen. It can run over 40 miles per hour and jump 40 feet horizontally. Adult males may have 100-square-mile territories. In 1879, Charles Sears, brother of La Honda founder John Sears, shot a mountain lion that was 7 feet in length while the lion was eating a young calf. (Courtesy U.S. Forest Service.)

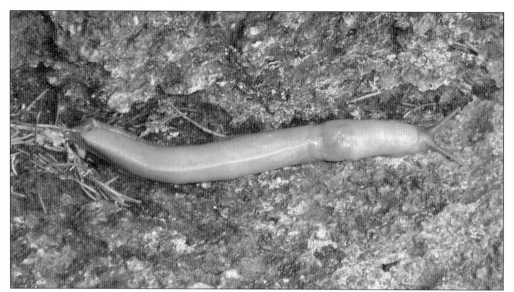

BANANA SLUGS (*ARIOLIMAX COLUMBIANUS*). The bright yellow Pacific banana slug seems ubiquitous in the shady, moist areas of La Honda. It is the second-largest species of slug in the world, growing over 9 inches long. Banana slugs excrete a thick coating of slime around their bodies that keeps their skin moist where respiration occurs. They remain inactive during the drier times of the year. A banana slug race was one of the activities of the annual La Honda Days celebrations of the 1960s and 1970s. The slug contestants had names like Acapulco Goldie, Mellow Yellow, and Goldilocks. (Courtesy author.)

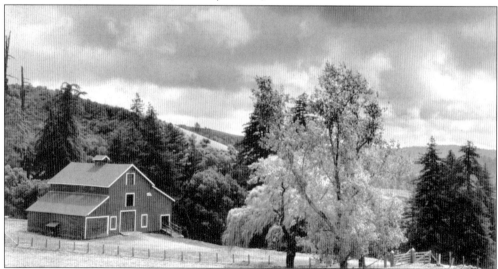

ENDANGERED AND THREATENED SPECIES. The Santa Cruz Mountains are rich in biological diversity and home to numerous endangered and threatened species. The pallid bat (*Antrozous pallidus*) is classified as a "species of concern" in the area and has its only known breeding site on the San Francisco Peninsula in the Red Barn, east of La Honda on Highway 84. This barn has also been the site of dances, junior rodeos, and community meetings for over 100 years. This barn is still one of the most photographed and painted locations in San Mateo County. The Red Barn was restored in 2002 but had to be done carefully so as not to impact the rare bat population there. (Courtesy Susan Friedman.)

NATURAL BEAUTY. La Honda is renowned for its natural beauty, the reason it attracted thousands of campers of the early 20th century. The opening of the San Francisco–Oakland Bay Bridge in 1936 and the Golden Gate Bridge in 1937 provided more opportunities for people in the area to go to other vacation spots, such as the Russian River in Sonoma County or Lake Tahoe. Today more motorcyclists than campers descend upon town during the summers. The waterfalls shown in the photograph is located in the Cuesta area of La Honda. (Courtesy Rob and Kathy [Zanone] Wolf.)

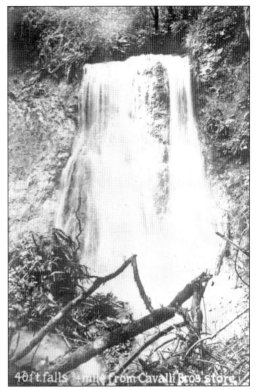

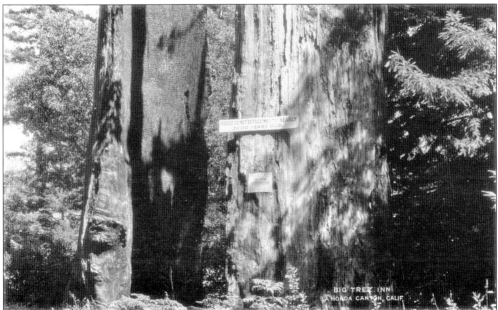

3,000-YEAR-OLD TREE, C. 1920. A sign attached to a redwood stump located at Big Tree Inn requested that visitors not deface a 3,000-year-old tree. Logging removed most of the more mature redwoods from the area by 1910, but even before logging, a tree this old in the La Honda area would have been rare. Ironically, the bottom sign on the tree appears to be a political advertisement. (Courtesy Charlie Catania.)

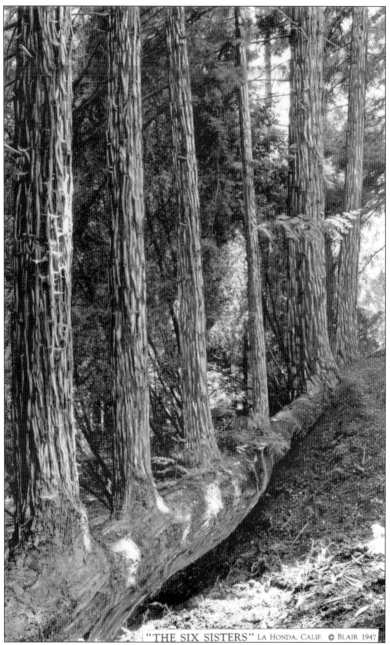

"THE SIX SISTERS" LA HONDA, CALIF. © BLAIR 1947

THE SIX SISTERS, 1947. The photograph shows The Six Sisters, which was group of six redwoods with heights from 60 to 100 feet that grew from a redwood tree that fell in the first half of the 20th century. A story about this tree's origin centers on a Spanish man named Don Ignacio Lineras, who had six beautiful daughters. Lineras fought against the Mexican governor and was imprisoned, but he eventually escaped and came to La Honda. One day, while his daughters were playing in the woods, an old woman appeared and began to entertain the girls until they lost track of time. Soon wild beasts surrounded their campfire, and the old woman told the girls to run across a fallen tree and she would save them. But the woman was really an evil enchantress who instead turned the girls into the Six Sisters. (Courtesy of Turk and Kim Borick.)

EARTHQUAKE COUNTRY.
La Honda is in a
precarious location about
halfway between the San
Gregorio Fault and the
infamous San Andreas
Fault, which runs along
the entire length of
San Mateo County and
caused extensive damage
in 1906. Other strong
earthquakes in La Honda
occurred in 1865, 1868,
and 1989 (the Loma
Prieta quake). La Honda
is in a prime location to
be heavily damaged by a
major earthquake, which
could isolate the town
from the rest of the Bay
Area. (Courtesy U.S.
Geological Survey.)

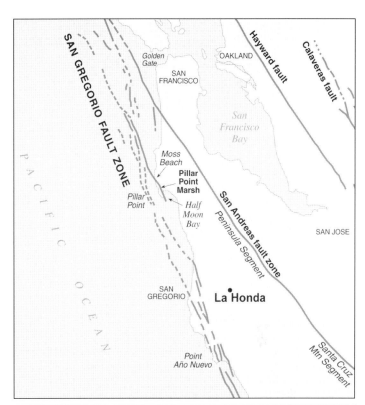

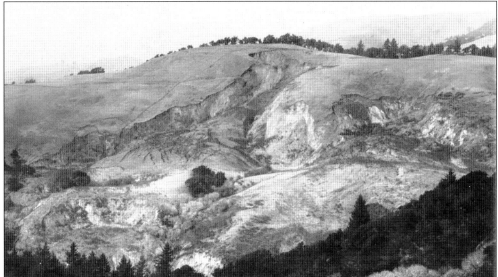

THE 1906 EARTHQUAKE. The 1906 earthquake triggered a massive mud slide in the La Honda hills on the Zanoni ranch near the top of Sears Ranch Road, as shown in this photograph. A California Earthquake Commission account of the damage in La Honda noted that "Plaster fell from the first floor walls in the Hotel La Honda, and 'lamps were all shaken off the tables, and all the chimneys were down.' Water also spilled from horse troughs, and a family's well-built ranch house with a strong frame structure was badly damaged." In nearby Bellvale, it continued, "a substantial landslide blocked the road." (Courtesy Milton Cavalli.)

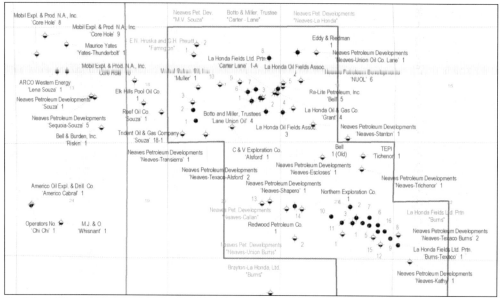

OIL! In 1921, A *San Mateo County Times* headline read, "La Honda District will be Exploited for Rich Oil Veins," and the oil boom started. In 1925, a La Honda oil well caught fire and the flames shot 50 feet in the air. This figure shows the large number of wells that have been drilled in the La Honda Oil Field. (Courtesy State of California, Department of Conservation.)

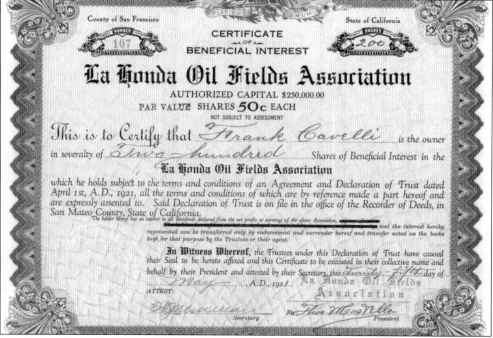

OIL STOCK, 1921. In 1926, the oil prospects looked so promising that there was a plan for building a pipeline from La Honda to a refinery in Redwood City. Although the pipeline wasn't built, the wells in La Honda had output over 1.2 million barrels of oil by 1979. The oil was pure, and a simple refinery near the wells in these early years sold gasoline for 9¢ a gallon. The photograph shows oil stock bought by Frank Cavalli in 1921. (Courtesy Milton Cavalli.)

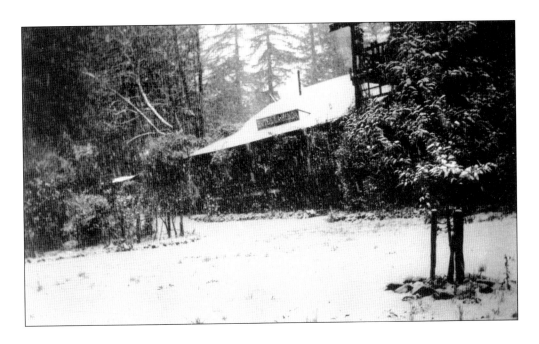

SNOW? Although snow is unusual in La Honda, which has an elevation of only about 400 feet, there have been a few notable years where heavy snow fell in town. The photograph above shows the Hotel La Honda in 1932 and the one on the bottom shows the Entrada bridge into Cuesta La Honda in 1972. Skyline Boulevard, just nine miles east of La Honda at a elevation of about 1,500 feet, gets some snow every couple of years, but even there the snow usually doesn't last more than a few days. A cold spell in 1949 froze Reflection Lake and broke water pipes throughout town. (Above courtesy Rob and Kathy [Zanone] Wolf; bottom courtesy Carol Cipriano.)

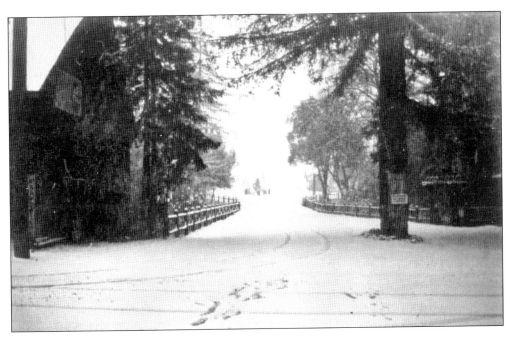

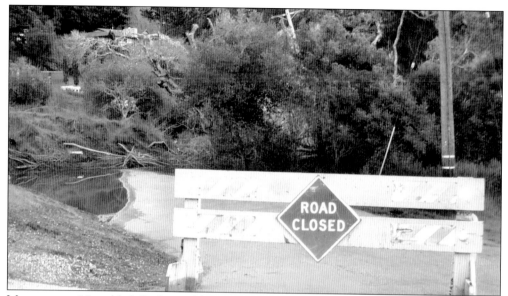

MUD SLIDES. Unstable hillsides and heavy rains in the Santa Cruz Mountains can become a destructive combination. In January 1862, rains created flash floods that destroyed half a dozen lumber mills in the nearby Santa Cruz Mountains. This photograph shows what is left of Scenic Drive in the Cuesta area after a massive mud slide during the El Nino winter of 1997–1998. This slide destroyed nine homes and is still moving, threatening more homes. San Mateo and other nearby counties were declared federal disaster areas in 1998 because of the slides and flooding caused by storms. (Courtesy author.)

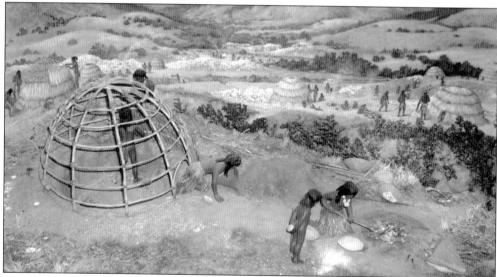

OHLONE INDIANS. Ohlone structures were typically made from willow branches and tule, as shown in this San Mateo County Historical Museum exhibit. The tules were bent into a dome-shaped frame, thatched with grass, and constructed over a shallow hole. The Ohlones' primary diet consisted of acorns and seeds, which were pounded into flour, and the bitterness was leached out before it was made into gruel or tamales. Ohlones were advanced in the art of basket weaving and design and were able to weave baskets so tight that they could hold water. Stones were heated and placed in these water-filled baskets as a way of cooking. (Courtesy author.)

Two

EARLY PIONEERS

In 1769, Capt. Don Gaspar de Portola led an expedition party of 63 men with 200 horses and mules; they were looking for Monterey Bay, which they had mistakenly passed. From October 24–26, the expedition rested for a few days near the mouth of San Gregorio Creek, because many of the party were sick or exhausted. Eleanor Freeman says in the book *Stories of San Mateo County* that some of these explorers traveled up the canyon toward Bellvale and La Honda.

The Ranchos of San Mateo County were under Mexican rule from 1822 to 1846. Cattle ranching, dairies, and farming dominated the economy during this era. La Honda fell in the area of Rancho San Gregorio, which was 17,783 acres given to Antonio Buelna of San Jose and Monterey. The Rancho was bounded on one side by Arroyo Hondo, the likely source of La Honda's present name.

The families and people mentioned in this chapter are just a small sampling of all the pioneers who built this town. Bud Foss, in his 1941 *History of La Honda*, lists the original pioneer families as: Weeks, John, Dubbs, Carter, Steinberg, Woodhams, Sears, Mendico, Rowley, Iverson, Rodgers, Palmer, Evans, Blomquist, McLeod, Bartley, Langley, Edwards, Wilbur, Dowd, Rich, Douglass, Monotti, Rapley, and Murphy.

The early La Honda days were interesting times with colorful people. One of these characters, for example, was Alexander Dowd. Before coming to La Honda in 1870, Alexander Dowd was looking for gold on the Stanislaus River and discovered the Calaveras Grove of Big Trees in the Sierra Nevada. He entertained people in La Honda with rattlesnake tricks until one bit his thumb, which then had to be amputated. In 1885, Dowd shot a grizzly bear, but it was still alive when he went over to skin it, and it bit off two of his fingers before it died.

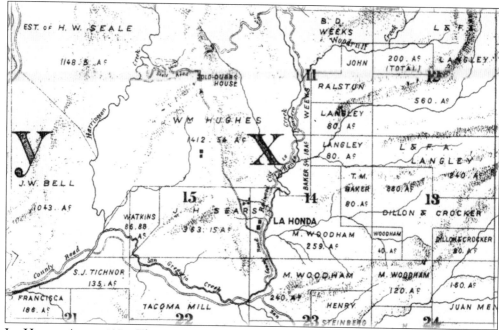

La Honda Area, 1879. This map shows the landowners around an early La Honda. The town had moved to its current location in 1877 and was still being built. The names on the map represent many of the earliest settlers who were historically important in the area. They include Bell, Sears, Woodhams, Steinberg, and Weeks. (Courtesy San Mateo County Historical Association.)

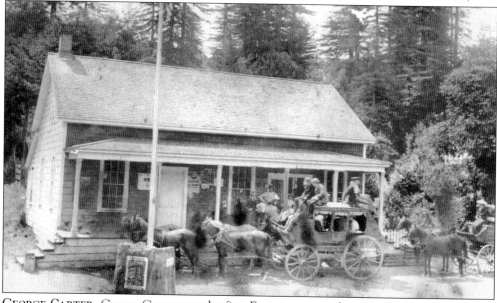

George Carter. George Carter was the first European to settle in the La Honda area, and in 1859, he built a water-powered mill on San Gregorio Creek, a mile from its junction with La Honda Creek. He rented out his house in what became Old La Honda to Andrew Sausman, who opened a store there. Shortly after Carter's house burned in 1880, the Carter family left the area. Carter cut down a redwood tree that ended up in front of the town store, as shown here; it was thereafter known as "Carter's Stump." (Courtesy Charlie Catania.)

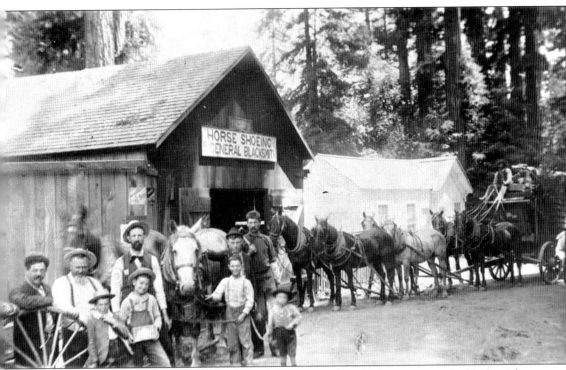

GROUP AT BLACKSMITH SHOP, 1894. In 1880, John Sears hired J. Lawrence as the blacksmith, but he then sold the shop to Isaac Davis in 1892. This photograph shows Bert Weeks, at left with his hand on the wheel and son Percy in front of him; Isaac Davis holding a hammer; and Ed George driving a load of tan bark. Tan bark was collected from a type of oak tree and was used for tanning hides. A Chinese washhouse for the mills, shown in the center of the photograph in a ghostly white, was located alongside the blacksmith shop. The blacksmith shop was converted into Applejack's saloon and the washhouse converted into a residence for the saloon's proprietor, "Applejack" Gabrielle. (Courtesy Bud Foss.)

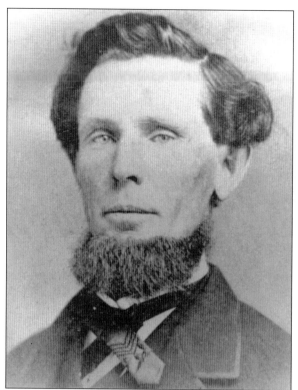

JOHN SEARS, 1870. In 1852, John Sears opened a popular hotel in what eventually was called Searsville, a former logging town near Woodside named after him. The Searsville area was turned into a reservoir around 1891 after the decline of the logging industry there. Sears bought 400 acres in the La Honda area and moved there in 1862. He bought the Sausman Store in Old La Honda but was later responsible for moving the town center from Old La Honda to its present location. (Courtesy Redwood City Library.)

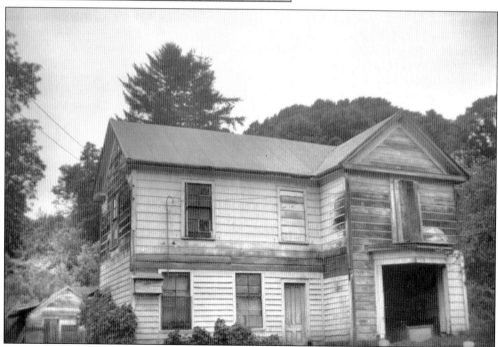

SEARS HOUSE, 1940. This is the original Sears House, built in 1863, as it looked in 1940. The house is located off Sears Ranch Road and has since been restored as a private residence. (Courtesy Bud Foss.)

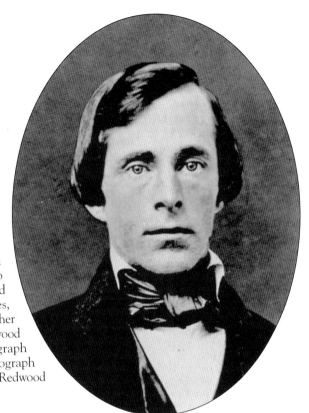

JOHN FAMILY, C. 1850. Burns John bought 1,500 acres of the San Gregorio grant in 1856 and then divided the land equally with Michael Dubbs for dairies, livestock, and raising wheat, hay, and other grains. These goods were carried to Redwood City along a horse trail. The photograph at right is Burns John, and the photograph below is of his wife, Martha. (Courtesy Redwood City Library.)

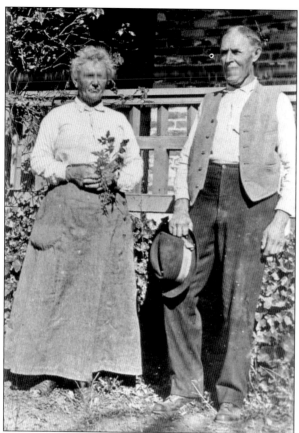

WEEKS FAMILY, C. 1910. Robinson J. Weeks purchased 2,300 acres of government land *c.* 1853 near La Honda for a dairy and farm. Weeks was contracted to build a road from La Honda Junction to San Gregorio, which was completed in 1872, the same year he was elected to be a county supervisor of the third district. On July 4, 1876, he celebrated his new Centennial Lumber Mill. On July 4, 1879, Robinson Weeks built an outdoor dance hall on his ranch to celebrate his appointment as a trustee of the La Honda School District. The photograph shows Robinson Weeks and his wife, Cordelia. (Courtesy Redwood City Library.)

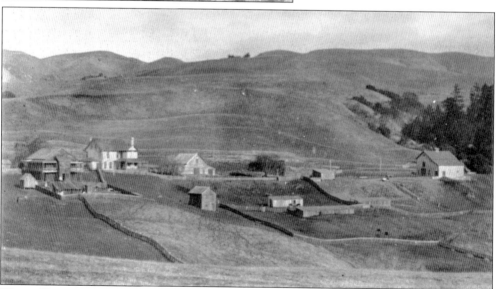

WEEKS RANCH, 1904. This photograph shows the new, white Weeks home in the left of the photograph. The old Weeks home is just to its left, and the famous Red Barn to its right. The Red Barn has hosted dances, rodeos, and community meetings over the past century. It has been restored and is located a few miles east of town on La Honda Road. (Courtesy Bud Foss.)

24

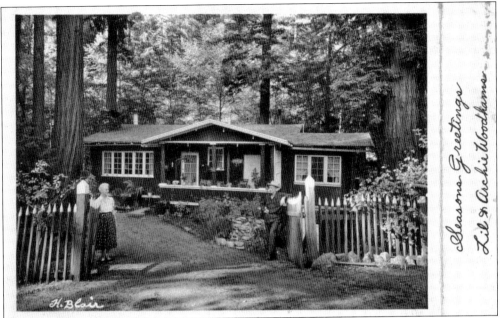

LIL AND ARCHIE WOODHAMS. Archie Woodhams was the son of Edgar Woodhams. Archie and his son Bud had an auto stage that hauled passengers and freight in the area. This holiday card showed their house, which still stands near where La Honda Park was once located. Several photographs in this book have the name Blair on them. Blair was a La Honda resident who photographed and reprinted vintage La Honda photographs in the 1940s. (Courtesy Rob and Kathy [Zanone] Wolf.)

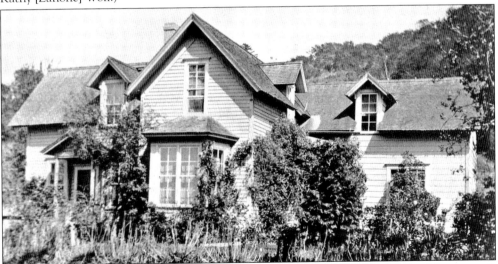

HOME OF JOSEPH AND MAURICE WOODHAMS. Joseph Woodhams and his brother Maurice each bought 240 acres in La Honda from the government about 1860. Maurice had four sons and was leader of the La Honda District Grange in 1874 and trustee for the La Honda School District in 1879. He built a house that took on guests during the summer months called the Glenside Ranch. The photograph shows this house built in 1879, which was located in the Cuesta La Honda area. The house was dismantled, and two houses were built from it, including the one shown in the photograph at the top of this page. (Courtesy Bud Foss.)

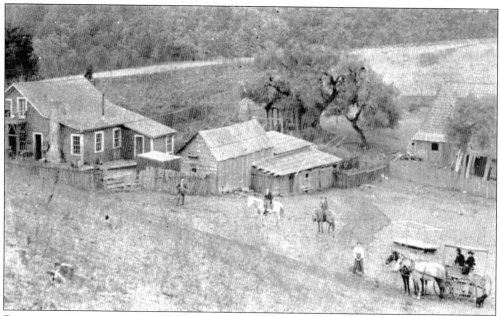

RODGERS RANCH, C. 1880. Benjamin Rodgers and his son Winfield moved to La Honda in 1867. He had four more children with Jane Williams: Ben Jr., Ceres, and two children who died in infancy. In December 1882, the children of Benjamin Rodgers threw dynamite in their stove, which blew up and slightly hurt them. The photograph shows the old Rodgers ranch buildings before they burned in 1883. (Courtesy Bud Foss.)

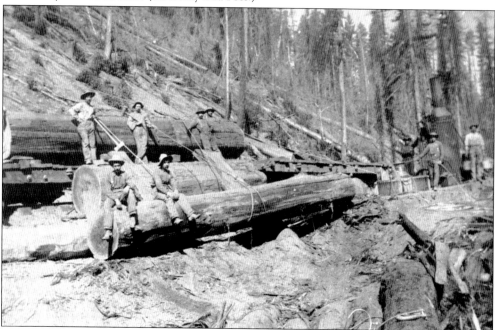

BEN RODGERS JR. Ben Rodgers Jr. was the son of Benjamin Rodgers, one of the first settlers in the La Honda area. Ben Rodgers Jr. is the rightmost person on the back log. The donkey engine shown on the right provided power through cables to move the logs. By 1900, these engines replaced much of the labor previously obtained from oxen. (Courtesy Bud Foss.)

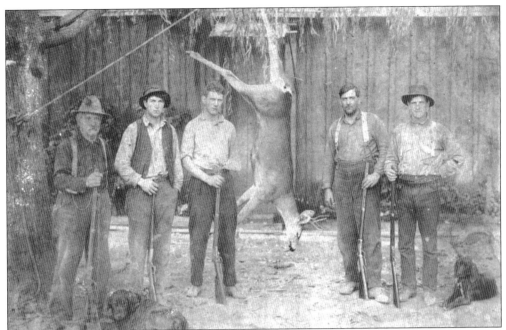

THE ZANONIS, C. 1916. James and Catherine Zanoni moved into the La Honda area as dairy farmers in the late 1800s. The Zanonis made flat cheese in 25-pound cakes. This photograph shows (from left to right) James Zanoni with sons Teddy, Armand, Matt, and Jimmy. Eighteen-year-old Armand, who had lost his arm in a threshing machine accident just a few weeks before this photograph was taken, shot the deer shown in the photograph. (Courtesy Rob and Kathy [Zanone] Wolf.)

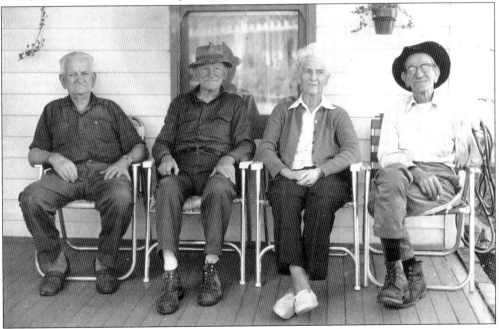

THE ZANONIS, C. 1970. Pictured from left to right are brothers Louie Zanoni and Gus Zanoni, sister Lil Woodhams, and brother Armand Zanone. They are sitting on the porch of Lil's house located in Cuesta La Honda. (Courtesy Rob and Kathy [Zanone] Wolf.)

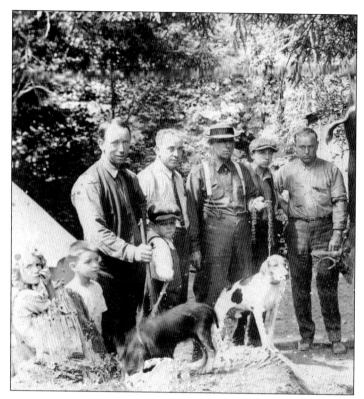

CAVALLI FAMILY, C. 1918. The Cavallis were involved in a number of stores, hotels, and saloons in La Honda. On a slow news day in 1917, a San Mateo newspaper reported, "Charles Cavalli of La Honda, where he is the proprietor of a general merchandise store, is under treatment for a badly wrenched back sustained Sunday while cranking his automobile." This photograph shows (from left to right) Gladys Cavalli, Milton Cavalli, Frank Cavalli, Jerry Towne, Charles Cavalli, Wes Bartley, Pete Towne, and Hubert Bartley. (Courtesy Milton Cavalli.)

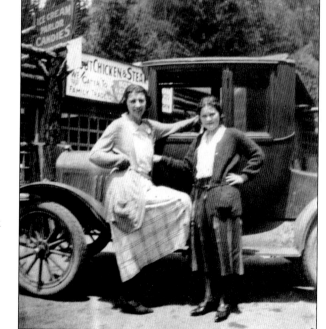

MARY CAVALLI, C. 1917. Mary "May" Cavalli (left), wife of Frank Cavalli, and friend Mary Sloan pose outside Bonzagni Lodge in front of a Model T Ford Coupe. Frank and brother Charles Cavalli were owners of Bonzagni Lodge at that time. (Courtesy Milton Cavalli.)

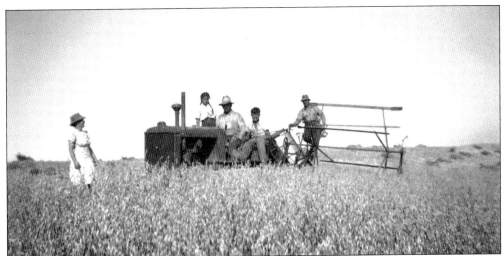

THE BORDIS. Antone "Babe" Bordi came to the Alpine area of La Honda around 1913. Antone drove hay for Mike Scarpa to where Moffett Field is now located in Mountain View. This trip took a full day of traveling each direction. This photograph shows binding grain on the Bartley Ranch. From left to right are: Antone Bordi's wife, Angela; Joanne Bordi; Joe Zanoni driving the Allis-Chalmers Model M tractor; Lou Bordi; and Antone Bordi on the binder. (Courtesy George and Mary Bordi.)

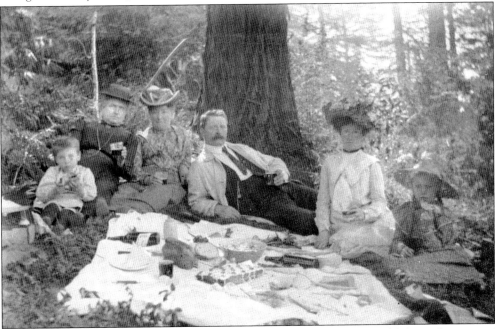

BELL FAMILY, C. 1900. The pioneer Bell family was instrumental in establishing the town of Bellvale, which was named after them. This photograph shows a family picnic of the Bell family. From left to right are Frank "Pat" Bell, two unidentified, Frank Bell, Ellen Rebecca "Becky" Palmer Bell, and Lottie Bell. Frank Bell owned the hotel in San Gregorio, and Lottie Bell died of appendicitis when she was 14 years old. Ellen Rebecca Bell was an only surviving child. Two of her siblings died in infancy, and four died during the La Honda diphtheria epidemic in the early 1880s. (Courtesy Mary and George Bordi.)

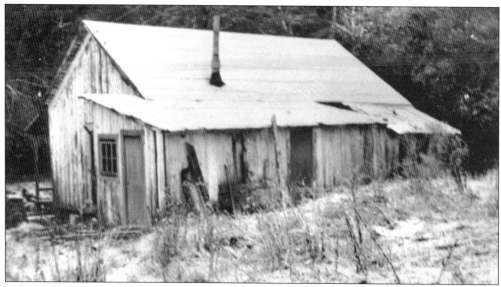

MALCOLM MCLEOD. Malcolm McLeod was an early pioneer who came to La Honda in 1868. He worked for the Templeton and Templeton Mill and then became a foreman at the Hanson Ackerson Mill. His two children attended the La Honda School in 1884. The photograph shows McLeod's rustic house in 1933. The house was built in 1869 and was later rented to blacksmith Isaac Davis. Milton Cavalli recalls tearing this building down and finding square nails, which were commonly used before 1880. (Courtesy Bud Foss.)

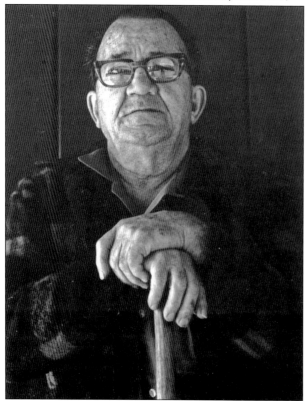

LATER PIONEERS. After a few generations, people like Basil Willett moved to La Honda. He owned much of the downtown La Honda area in the 1970s, including the post office, Baw's Fine Foods, and the old general store. Baw stood for Basil A. Willett. The restaurant had a jukebox and the best hamburgers in town. (Courtesy Susan Friedman.)

Three

OLD LA HONDA
AND BELLVALE

Old La Honda was located at the junction of La Honda Creek and San Gregorio Creek, less than a mile west of the present location of La Honda. Andrew Sausman opened a store there in 1868. Since there was no road to the summit where he stored supplies at his ranch, he had to carry them down by horseback. In 1872, John Sears bought half interest in Sausman's store, and it was enlarged at that point. The new Redwood City–Pescadero road opened that year, which made it easier to get supplies to the store from Redwood City. In 1873, a post office was opened in Old La Honda. The Knight's Stage Company had the contract to bring the mail there, and Andrew Sausman was made the first postmaster.

During the July Fourth celebration in town in 1877, William Sears (John's son) announced that he was going to move his store three-quarters of a mile up the road to near the old bear pit. A bear pit was a large hole where a grizzly bear and bull were put together to fight as a kind of entertainment for some of the early settlers. The bear pit may have been located under the blackberry patch next to where Pioneer Market is located today. The name "La Honda" moved with Sears to its present location. An 1877 newspaper mentioned that the new town site was being prepared "in order to clear a site for the new buildings forty splendid redwoods were felled." Within a few years, there was not only a store, but also a hotel, school, post office, and blacksmith shop located there.

In 1868, Bellvale was chosen as the headquarters of a newly formed school district that included what are now La Honda, Pescadero, and the Coastside Union school districts. The next year, a generous Bellvale farmer, James Bell, paid for a schoolhouse and a teacher for the first year. The round-trip distance for La Honda students to go to the Bellvale School each day was about eight miles. Most children walked, although some had horses. Bellvale eventually lost its school and post office; it no longer exists as a separate town.

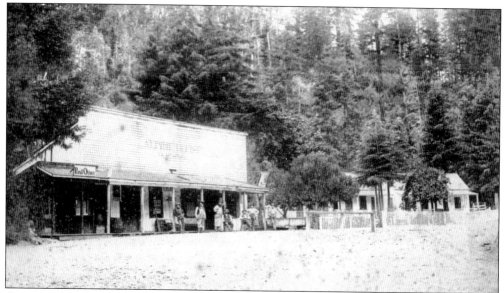

ORIGINAL STORE AND POST OFFICE, C. 1875. The original store, first run by Sausman and later by Sears, is shown. The photograph was probably taken between 1873 and 1877, the years that the post office was still located in Old La Honda. The store was primarily run by Armand Kieffer. Armand Kieffer had two other brothers: August "Gus" and Valentine. The original La Honda Post Office can be seen on the left of the building. The words "Alpine House"—and below that "La Honda"—appear faded on the front of the building. (Courtesy Mary and George Bordi.)

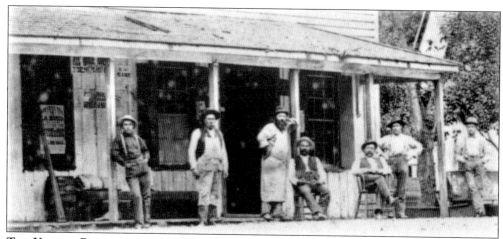

THE KIEFFER BROTHERS, C. 1875. In 1893, Armand and Gus Kieffer built a saloon, cottages, and a dance hall at the original Sausman's store site. Every Saturday night during the summer, they would have a dance at their dance hall. Their hotel was also well known for its Bastille Day celebrations, a tradition continued later at Bonzagni Lodge. Armand and Gus Kieffer are the two men standing near the front door. (Courtesy Mary and George Bordi.)

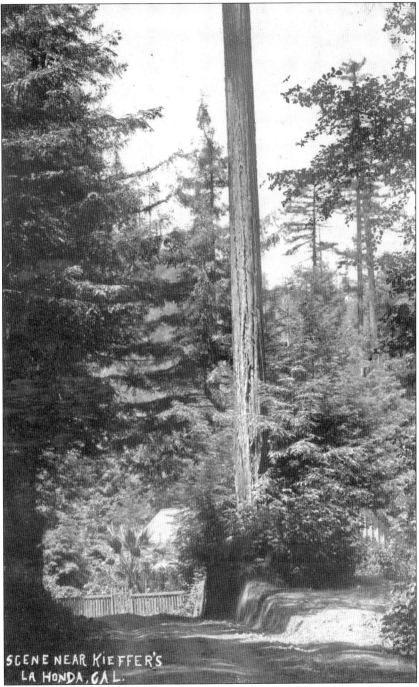

SCENE NEAR KIEFFER'S
LA HONDA, CAL.

"SCENE NEAR KIEFFER'S." This photograph was taken just outside of the Kieffer resort area. The top of the building and palm trees are visible near the bottom of the photograph. Old La Honda never recovered from the town moving to its new location in 1877, and eventually the Kieffer resort closed down. In 1897, Gus Kieffer died after being thrown by a team of horses he was driving. In 1915, Valentine Kieffer killed himself with a shotgun, and brother Armand died the following year. (Courtesy Rob and Kathy [Zanone] Wolf.)

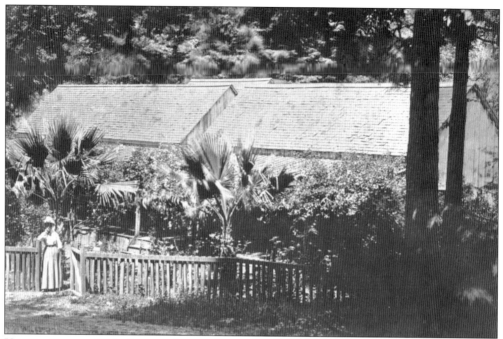

KIEFFER RESORT. This photograph was taken in front of the Kieffer resort, showing a closer view. Notice the characteristic palm trees planted there. (Courtesy Bud Foss.)

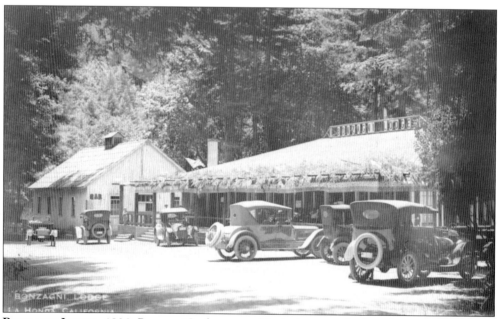

BONZAGNI LODGE, 1920. Bonzagni Lodge, named for its host, was built at the site of the Kieffer resort. Although deserted for a while, Bonzagni Lodge was eventually bought by Frank Cavalli in 1912. The left side of Bonzagni Lodge was the saloon, the middle was the dining room, and the right side was the dance hall with a stage. (Courtesy Mary and George Bordi.)

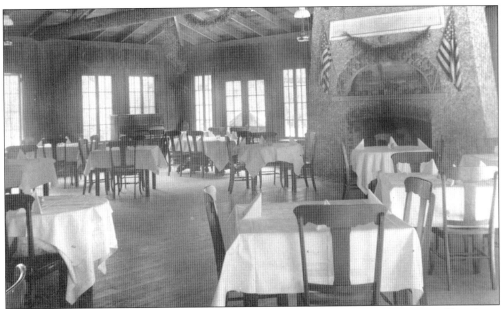

INSIDE BONZAGNI LODGE, 1926. Bonzagni Lodge had a spacious dining area warmed by a huge stone fireplace. In 1919, celebrating the Bastille tradition started by the Kieffer brothers, Bonzagni Lodge advertised the following: "A splendid chicken dinner for $1.00. A five piece band will furnish music for the dance in the evening." In 1926, the *Redwood City Standard* reported that the Fourth of July has been celebrated in La Honda for several generations and that "many of the prominent citizens of San Mateo County make their plans months ahead to attend this particular celebration." (Courtesy Milton Cavalli.)

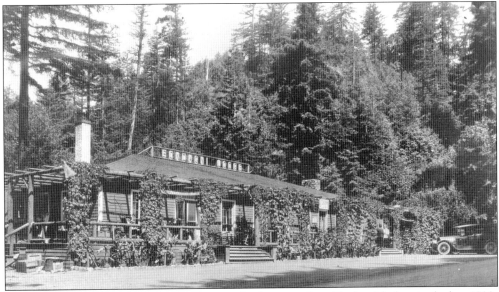

BONZAGNI'S ROSE BUSHES, C. 1922. Bonzagni Lodge started as a blacksmith shop in the late 1800s and was converted into a bar and restaurant in the 1920s. Legend claims that it was a bordello and speakeasy during Prohibition and that tunnels connected it to cabins in the area for storage of whiskey for other speakeasies on the peninsula. This lodge was also known for having one of the largest and oldest rose bushes in Northern California. (Courtesy Turk and Kim Borick.)

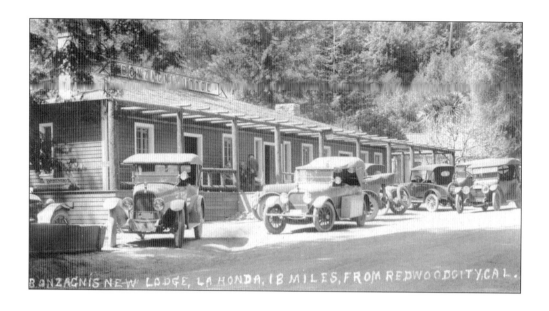

BANDITS AT BONZAGNI LODGE. On April Fool's Day in 1917, a fake hold-up was staged by an armed and masked man on one of the employees at Bonzagni Lodge. The lodge burnt down in 1922 and was rebuilt the next year, but Bonzagni died shortly after its reopening. (Above courtesy Milton Cavalli; below courtesy Charlie Catania.)

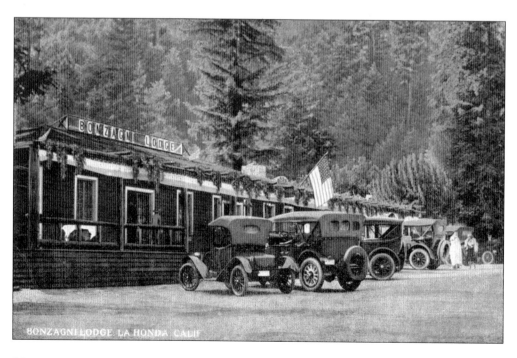

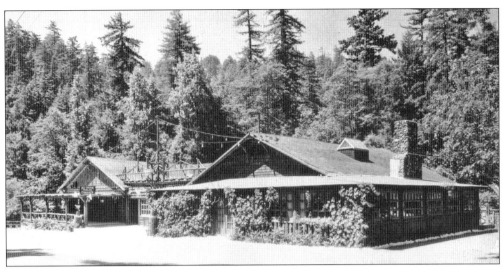

BLOWING UP BONZAGNI LODGE. After passing through several hands, Tony Fodera took over Bonzagni Lodge in 1931 but had a different plan for it after a couple of years. He planted 36 sticks of dynamite to blow up the lodge to collect the insurance money. The dynamite failed to go off, but he was caught and sent to prison for six months. In the 1940s, the Catholic Church held Sunday services in Bonzagni Lodge, until a church was built on Sears Ranch Road. (Courtesy Charlie Catania.)

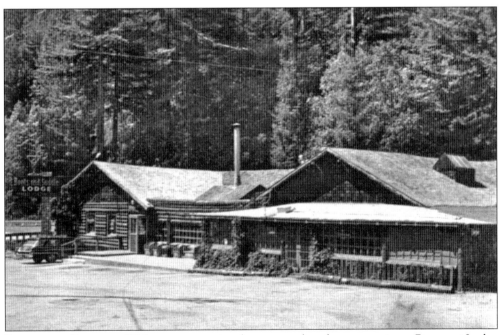

BOOTS AND SADDLES. Without many major changes—other then a new sign—Bonzagni Lodge turned into Boots and Saddles Lodge around 1945. The local residents just referred to the lodge as "Boots." Local resident Neil Young sometimes played there unannounced in the 1970s. The bar was destroyed by fire in 1984 after a number of other mysterious fires occurred in the area. (Courtesy Hayden Coggins.)

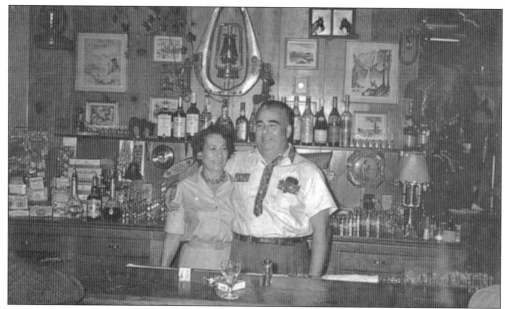

BOOTS OWNERS, THE MCCARTYS, C. 1950. The back of this postcard reads, "Grace and Mac McCarty—owners and operators of the Boots and Saddles Lodge amidst California's magnificent redwoods at La Honda in San Mateo Co., California. Wonderful food and unique surroundings make this a very popular resort. Closed January 1 to April 1." This photograph shows Grace and Mac behind their bar. (Courtesy Milton Cavalli.)

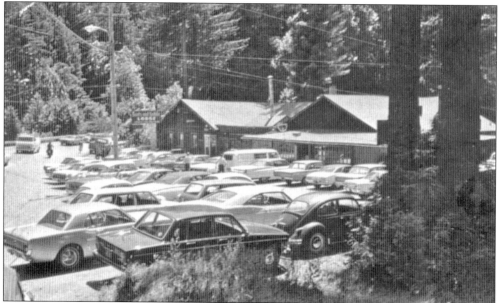

BUSY DAY AT BOOTS. Mac McCarty acquired the rundown Bonzagni Lodge and created Boots and Saddles. Mac had been a professional bassist with the San Francisco Symphony, and until the 1960s, Boots and Saddles was known for its Saturday afternoon jazz concerts. It had a family-friendly atmosphere and was the locals' destination for birthdays, anniversaries, and other family events. As this photograph shows, Boots and Saddles often drew a large crowd. (Courtesy Hayden Coggins.)

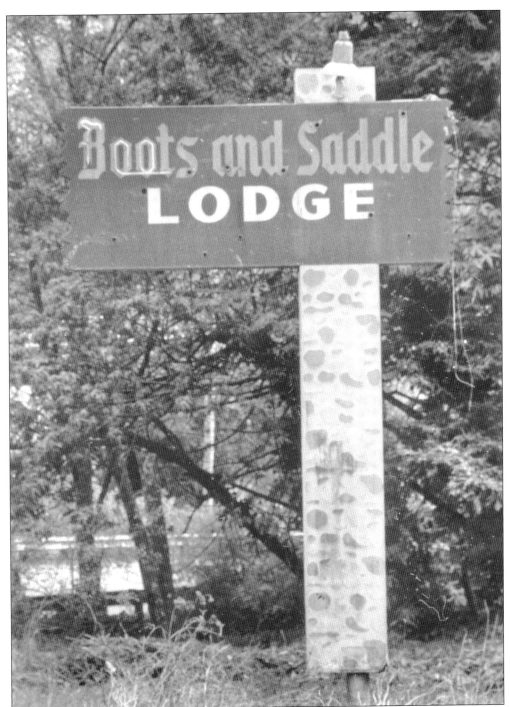

Boots and Saddles Sign. For years after the tragic fire in 1984 that destroyed Boots and Saddles, this sign was only reminder of what once was there. Although the community rallied around resurrecting Boots, the lodge was never rebuilt. Strict county requirements for increased parking have been given as one reason that prevented reconstruction. The county also pressured for this sign to be removed, and it is no longer there. (Courtesy Brook Tankle.)

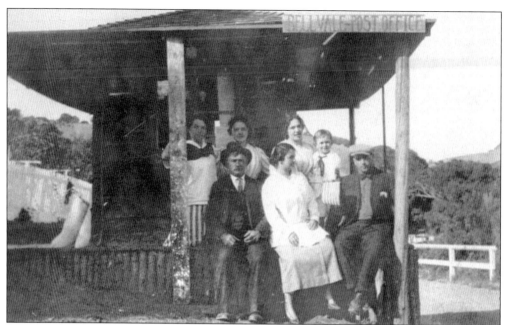

BELLVALE POST OFFICE. The Bellvale Post Office was established in 1897 with Postmaster James W. Bell. In 1904, Lilia E. Bell became postmaster, but the post office was closed in 1922, with mail going to La Honda because there were only two addresses left in Bellvale. Pictured from left to right are the following: (first row) John Souza; Louise Souza, and Ed Fischer; (second row) Angie Souza, Annie Souza, Lena Souza, and Norman Souza. (Courtesy Mary and George Bordi.)

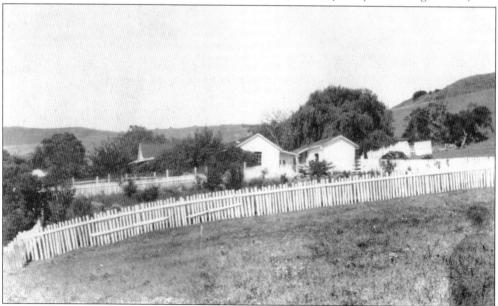

OIL AT THE BELL RANCH. In 1875, a rich cinnabar mine was discovered in Bellvale, and in 1895, oil was found. In 1895, the *Redwood City Democrat* noted this about Bell's Ranch: "Indications are that his ranch covers one of the richest oil deposits on the coast." On one part of the ranch, oil was bubbling up out of the ground and running into San Gregorio Creek. (Courtesy Milton Cavalli.)

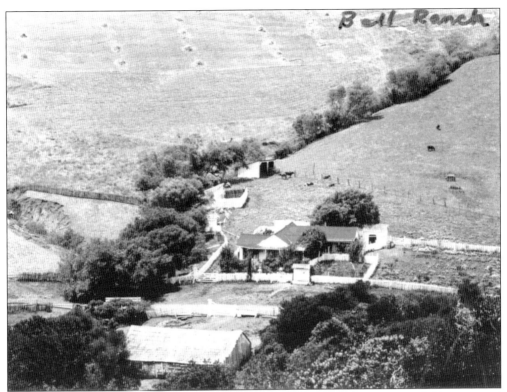

BELL RANCH. A 1902 *Redwood City Democrat* advertisement for vacationers read, "A sunny and homelike farm house situated on the banks of the San Gregorio creek; pleasant, healthy, and ease of access. The best home cooking. Rates $5 per week. For particulars address: Mrs L. E. Bell, Bellvale, Cal." The Bell Ranch eventually burned down. (Both courtesy Milton Cavalli.)

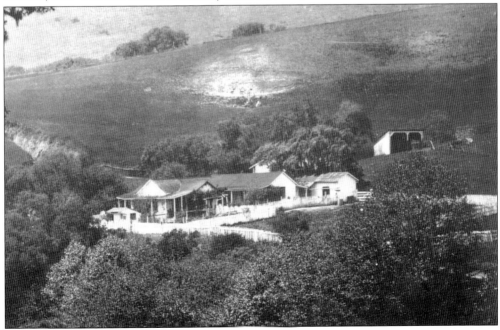

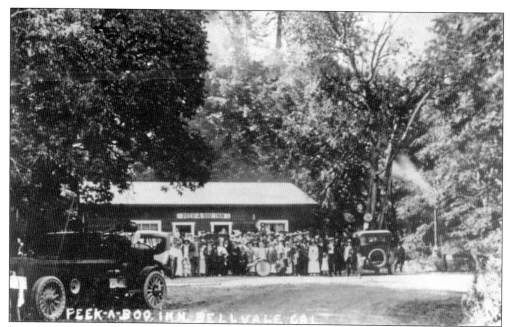

BELLVALE'S PEEK-A-BOO INN. This inn, operated by Louis Zanoni, was located just off La Honda road in the now-vanished town of Bellvale. The left side was a dance hall, the right side was a bar, and in the back was a kitchen. Behind the inn were cabins for campers. In 1916, Peek-a-Boo advertised a barbecue, charging 25¢ per person. On April 11, 1923, three bandits in a Hudson car held up Peek-a-Boo Inn and got away with $100. The inn has since burned down. (Courtesy Rob and Kathy [Zanone] Wolf.)

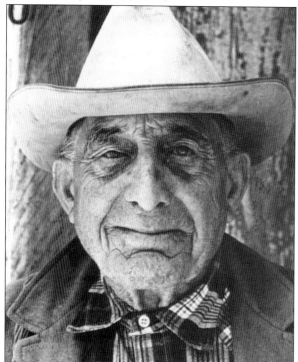

"THE LAST RESIDENT OF BELLVALE." Frank Anzar was called the last resident of Bellvale in Charles Jones's 1974 book, *A Separate Place*. Anzar was an expert with horses, and at least once he rode his horse inside the Boots and Saddles Lodge. Anzar also drove herds of stock over long distances in the 1920s. (Courtesy Susan Friedman.)

Four

DAYS OF BANDITS
AND LOGGERS

Although most construction in the Spanish-Mexican era was in adobe, timber was still required for the supporting beams. By the 1790s, the forests near present-day Woodside and Portola Valley provided this lumber. The first products were handmade shingles and hand-cut logs and lumber.

Destruction of the forests occurred quickly in the years following the arrival of the early pioneers. By 1859, this area had at least eight sawmills and three shingle mills. Identifying the history of the subsequent mills is difficult. Mills would frequently move, burn down, change hands, or rebuild under new names or partners. By 1870, the best timber had been removed from the eastern slopes of the Sierra Morena, the Spanish and Mexican name for the eastern slopes of the Santa Cruz Mountains. Logging then started to move west over the Santa Cruz Mountains toward La Honda.

The early pioneer years were plagued with a lack of law enforcement. Bandits were known to roam and hide out in the Santa Cruz Mountains, including the La Honda area. Joaquin Murrietta and his gang and Sontag and Evans, who liked to hold up Southern Pacific Railroads, hid out in the nearby mountains. Although these names have now become obscure, the Younger brothers, who were members of the Jesse James gang, hid in La Honda and are still remembered as notorious criminals of this era.

One more recent crime of some notoriety was the Log Cabin Ranch well murder. In the 1920s, a woman who lived by what is now the Log Cabin Ranch killed her husband with her boyfriend and threw his body down a well. A neighbor saw them filling up the well and mentioned it to others around town who discovered the husband was missing. The woman and her boyfriend were caught and sent to jail for the murder.

Another odd crime took place in 1949 involving a woman nicknamed "Bubbles." Bubbles was caught forging checks and later trying to break into a La Honda cabin. As she was being booked on the forged check charge, the jailer discovered her true gender after she was required to remove her clothes before being imprisoned. Bubbles was actually a transgendered man named Wilhelm Von Stokke, who had been living as a woman for 16 years around La Honda, working as a babysitter and housekeeper.

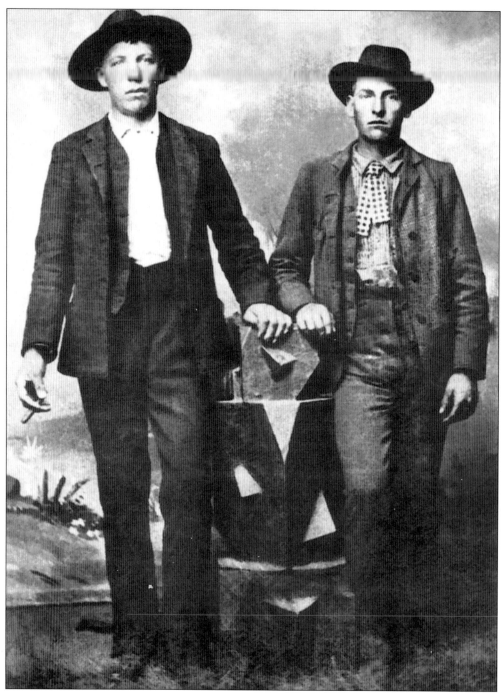

YOUNGER BROTHERS. This photograph shows Cole and Jim Younger. The Younger brothers had a ruthless reputation. It was said that during the Civil War, Cole Younger stacked several Yankee prisoners in front of a tree to see how many bodies his rifle's bullet would penetrate. The Younger brothers, Cole, Jim, and Bob, were part of Jesse James's infamous gang, and they changed their names and hid from the law at the Ray Ranch in La Honda in the 1860s. Jim Younger took on the name Hardin, while brother Cole used the alias Parsons. (Courtesy Redwood City Library.)

LAST ROBBERY FOR THE YOUNGERS. Jesse James's plan was to rob the Northfield, Minnesota, bank, which is the building on the far right with the arched windows, and then escape over the iron bridge spanning the Cannon River. However, on September 7, 1876, this final robbery went very wrong for the Youngers. Jesse James evaded capture for this robbery, but the Youngers were caught by a posse several days later. (Courtesy Redwood City Library.)

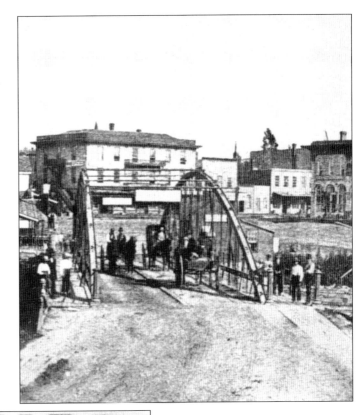

REWARD!
- DEAD OR ALIVE -

$5,000.00 will be paid for the capture of the men who robbed the bank at

NORTHFIELD, MINN.

They are believed to be Jesse James and his Band, or the Youngers.

All officers are warned to use precaution in making arrest. These are the most desperate men in America.

Take no chances! Shoot to kill!!

J. H. McDonald,

WANTED—JESSE JAMES AND THE YOUNGERS. Jim Younger was wounded in the shoulder and jaw during the get-away, and after several days, Jesse and his brother Frank deserted the Younger brothers. The posse that finally caught up with the Youngers did additional damage to them, including 11 bullet wounds for Cole alone. However all the Youngers survived, and they were sent to Minnesota's Stillwater Penitentiary. (Courtesy Redwood City Library.)

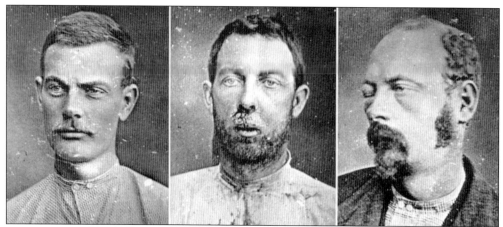

THE YOUNGERS AFTER THEIR CAPTURE. These photographs show (from left to right) Bob, Jim, and Cole Younger just after their capture. Bob died of tuberculosis in prison in 1889. Jim was paroled in 1901, but because his parole terms forbade him to marry his fiancé, Alix Mueller, he committed suicide in 1902. Cole wrote a memoir that portrayed himself as more of a Confederate avenger than the outlaw that he was. After Cole Younger was released in 1901, he toured with Jesse James's brother, Frank, in a Wild West show. Cole Younger died in 1916. (Courtesy Redwood City Library.)

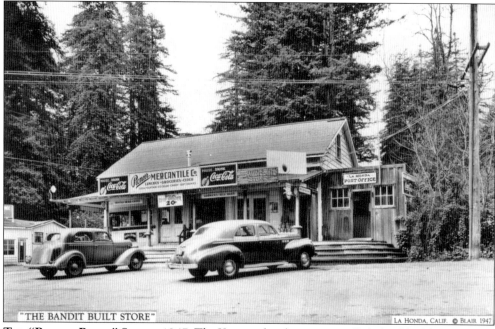

THE "BANDIT BUILT" STORE, 1947. The Younger brothers supposedly helped build the original Sears store, pictured. However, the story of the "bandit built" Sears store is improbable because the Youngers were already in prison in the summer of 1876 for the Northfield bank robbery before the store was built the following year. Although the story is dubious, it was probably good for business, as evidenced by the sign in the photograph. Another tall tale was given to a *Half Moon Bay Review* reporter in the 1960s who wrote in an article that Jesse James once owned the James Hotel in La Honda. (Courtesy Rob and Kathy [Zanone] Wolf.).

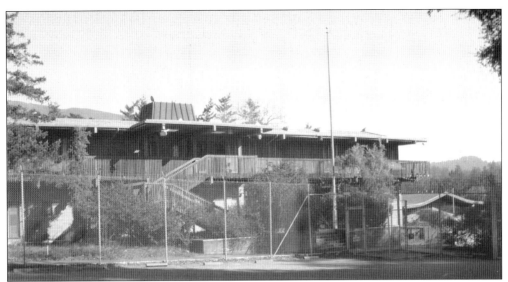

JUVENILE DETENTION CAMPS. Several juvenile detention camps are still located within a few miles of La Honda. The Log Cabin Ranch School, established by the County of San Francisco in 1942, was for 15- to 18-year-old offenders. A similar facility called Hidden Valley Ranch opened in 1969 and was for 11- to 14-year-old offenders. A separate facility for San Mateo juveniles is the Glenwood Boys Ranch, which opened in 1962 and, according to a newspaper account of the time, was for boys to "get custody, care and discipline similar to that which competent parents would provide." This photograph is of the Honor Camp, a low-security facility for San Mateo County adult men that is now closed down. Boy Scout Camp Pomponio was located at this scenic location before the Honor Camp was built. (Courtesy author.)

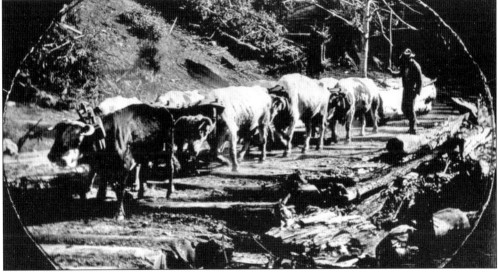

EARLY LOGGING, 1865. The legend of the "bandit built" store was based on interviews of La Honda residents Oscar John and Walter Ray and conducted by San Mateo County historian Roscoe Wyatt. The Younger brothers passed themselves off as cousins of a local family, the Johns, and worked at the Ray ranch. John and Ray both claimed they saw the Younger brothers building the Sears Store in La Honda. The photograph shows Walter Ray with a whip and an oxen team pulling logs over a skid row. (Courtesy Bud Foss.)

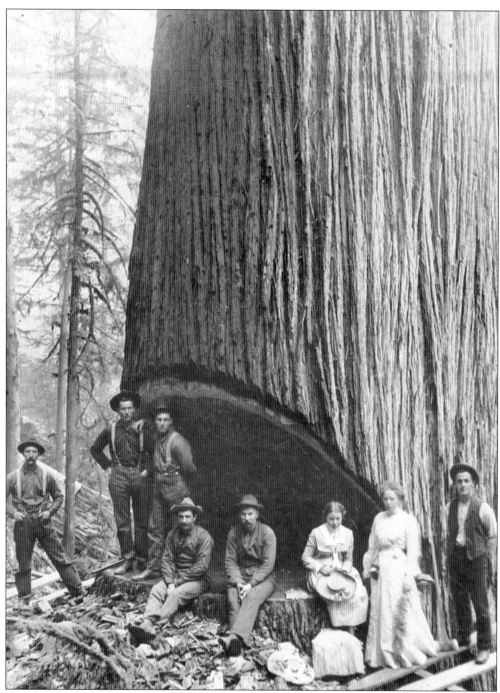

FELLING THE TREE, 1904. It is difficult to appreciate the work of the lumbermen working without modern equipment—a tree had to be felled; barkers trimmed the trees and peeled the bark; bucking the tree involved cutting it into manageable lengths; and logs were gathered at a central place and then transported to a mill to be cut and stacked. Each step required different skills and posed different dangers. Ben Rodgers Jr., son of pioneer Benjamin Rodgers, is fourth from left. (Courtesy Bud Foss.)

SKID ROAD. The skid road, sometimes lubricated with animal fat, was created to help provide support and reduce friction for logs while they were being moved. The stench from this rancid fat was sometimes overwhelming. A saying at the time was that the smell was so strong that the logs could float down the hill on the fumes alone. (Courtesy Kim and Turk Borick.)

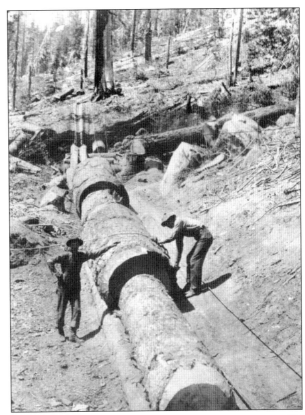

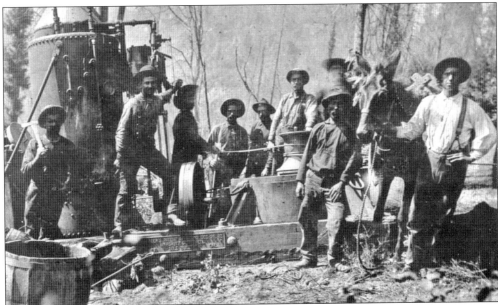

DONKEY ENGINES AND WORKERS AT CALIFORNIA MILL. A donkey engine, also known as a steam donkey, was a type of stationary steam engine used to haul logs to a log landing. Logs were pulled with a wire cable attached to a winch. By 1900, donkey engines had replaced the need for most of the oxen. Ben Rodgers Jr. is fifth from left. (Courtesy Bud Foss.)

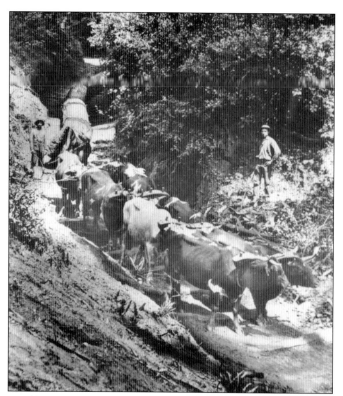

HAULING LOGS TO WOODRUFF MILL, C. 1902. Ed Sallewager (left) and Charles Wyman bring logs to Woodruff Mill. Woodruff Mill was located about a mile east of town on La Honda Road, where Woodruff Creek flows into La Honda Creek. Oxen were used in the woods, but horses were used on the roads because they were faster. This photograph was taken by local resident Gus Zanoni. (Courtesy Bud Foss.)

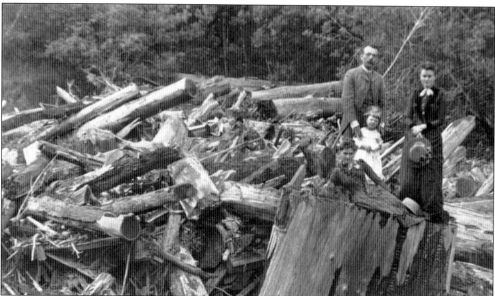

MILL SCRAP PILE AND FAMILY, 1884. The photograph shows a scrap pile at the Hanson Ackerson and Company Mill. Lumber was cut here for Ferdinand de Lesseps's attempted canal in Panama. Hanson Ackerson and Company bought many of the mills in the area to almost create a monopoly on lumber. The photograph shows from left to right Tillie Pringle, Willie White, H. White, and Elizabeth Pringle. The Pringle sisters were both schoolteachers in the area. (Courtesy Bud Foss.)

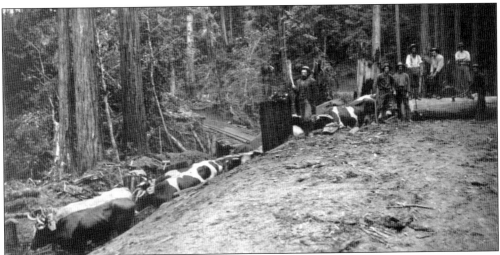

HANSON ACKERSON AND COMPANY, 1884. Hanson Ackerson and Company purchased and moved a preexisting mill to the La Honda Creek headwaters in Deer Gulch in 1865. It shut down in 1871, when lumber prices dropped too low to be profitable, but started up again the following year. The lumber was then shipped out from a wharf that Hanson Ackerson and Company owned in Redwood City. In 1879, the mill was moved about a mile farther down the creek. The photograph shows Charlie Townsend, bull whacker, with a switch in his hand. (Courtesy Bud Foss.)

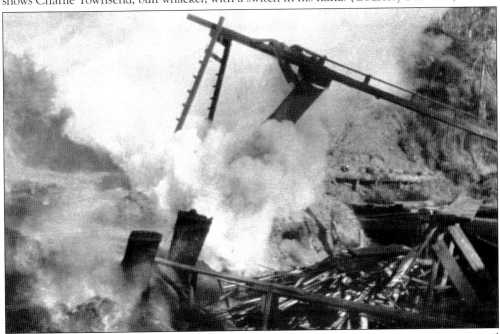

WOODRUFF MILL, C. 1902. Bert and Asa Weeks returned from the Washington Territory and opened the Woodruff Mill at the junction of Woodruff and La Honda Creeks in 1896. Timber was hauled down from the upper end of Woodruff Gulch by bull whacker Ed Sallewager or Walter Ray. In 1901, after nearby timber was exhausted, the operation was moved about 500 yards upstream of the earlier Centennial Mill on La Honda Creek. The mill was then moved to Pescadero Creek, where Bert Weeks owned 160 acres. This photograph shows the sawdust elevator and scrap pile. (Courtesy Bud Foss.)

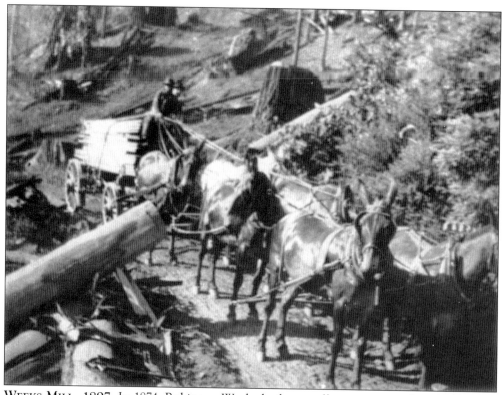

WEEKS MILL, 1897. In 1874, Robinson Weeks built a small, water-powered sawmill called Centennial Mill on La Honda Creek. He converted it to steam the following year. His sons Bert and Asa took over the mill operations when Robinson Weeks was appointed to county supervisor. The photograph shows William Douglass Jr. hauling lumber from Weeks mill below Weeks dairy. (Courtesy Bud Foss.)

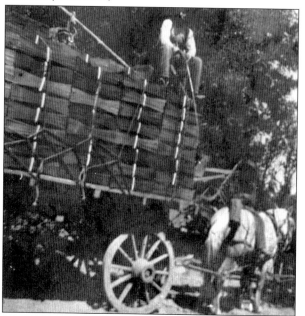

HASKINS AND SONS SHINGLE MILLS. This mill was built by J. W. Haskins and was located on a tributary of Pescadero Creek. In 1873, James Coates caught his foot in the mill's machinery, which pulled him in and crushed him to death. In 1874, the mill burned to the ground but was rebuilt the following year. In 1875, William Milliken's coat was caught in the machinery, but he was able to jerk loose from his clothes. After it was over, Milliken was on the ground with only his boots left on him. This photograph shows Joe Felix sitting on the shingles, and Morris Felix sitting on the white horse hauling shingles from the mill to Redwood City. (Courtesy Bud Foss.)

Five

COMMERCE AND INDUSTRY

Before and after the logging boom, the La Honda area supported ranching, dairies, and farming. Some entrepreneurs also removed ferns, redwood burls, and other plants from the forest to bring back to sell in the cities.

A post office was approved and constructed in 1873 in Old La Honda, however it was moved to new La Honda in 1878. Franklin Todd rented the store in Old La Honda and petitioned the Redwood City postmaster to bring the post office back to Old La Honda but was turned down in 1880. He had to give up the store and died the next year.

In 1868, Bellvale was chosen as the headquarters of a school district that included La Honda. The round-trip distance for La Honda students to go to Bellvale each day was about eight miles. Some of the La Honda residents had a plan to make it easier for the La Honda children to get to school. Maurice Woodhams had managed to gain control of the school district's board of trustees in 1871. One evening in the summer of 1871, some of the La Honda board members went unannounced to the Bellvale School. They loaded their wagons up with desks, tables, chairs, and books and brought them to La Honda. The Bellvale residents were understandably furious and complained to the county board of supervisors. The county officials attempted to resolve the problem by dividing the school district in half—one district included the Bellvale School and the other the La Honda school.

The La Honda schoolhouse held classes for 81 years afterward, although it did suspend operations in 1874 because of a lack of funds. The school's last year in service was in 1952, when the one-room school became clearly inadequate for La Honda's 79 students. A new school was built on Sears Ranch Road. The old Bell schoolhouse in Bellvale was torn down in 1963, making the La Honda schoolhouse the oldest in San Mateo County.

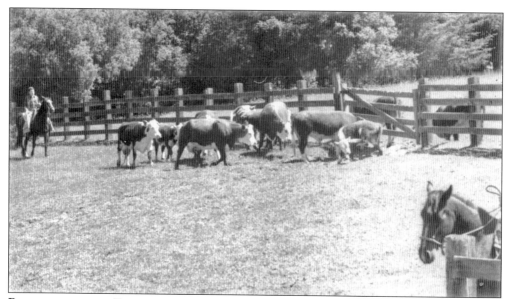

RANCHING AT THE TOWNE RANCH, C. 1968. This photograph shows the last roundup for the branding of Kendall Bartley "Pete" Towne's cattle in the Alpine area of La Honda. The ranch was sold and is now called the Jack Brooks Horse Camp, which is part of Sam McDonald Park. Pete Towne founded Towne Ford in Redwood City. Shortly before his death in 1992, Pete Towne wrote a collection of memoirs of La Honda called *Forget-Me-Not Under the Redwoods*. (Courtesy George and Mary Bordi.)

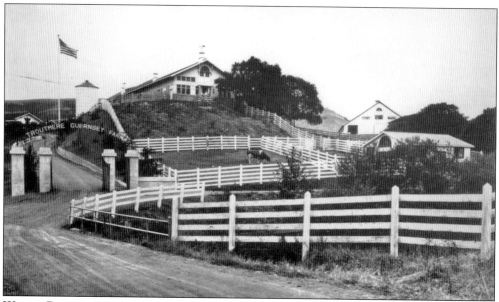

WORLD-RECORD MILK PRODUCER. In 1930, the *San Mateo Times* reported, "Topsy, prize cow of the Troutmere Guernsey Farm, La Honda, was yesterday awarded the crown as the world's greatest milk producing Guernsey. In 1929, Topsy produced 23,152 pounds of milk and 935 pounds of butter fat, totaling 23 times her own weight." The Troutmere cattle were all purebred Guernseys, meaning their ancestry could be traced back to the original stock from the Channel Islands in England. (Courtesy Charlie Catania.)

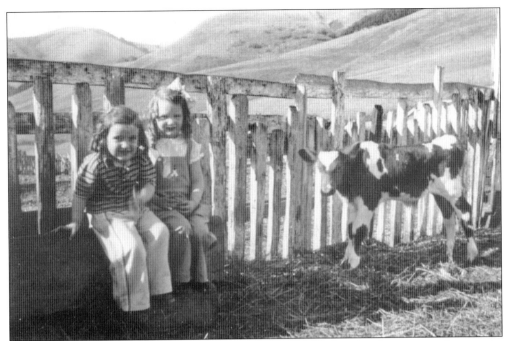

DAIRIES, 1940. Sometimes ranchers and dairy farmers joke that they have more photographs of their favorite and prize animals than they do of their own children. This local photograph may have been a compromise, instead of having to choose between the two. (Courtesy Rob and Kathy [Zanone] Wolf.)

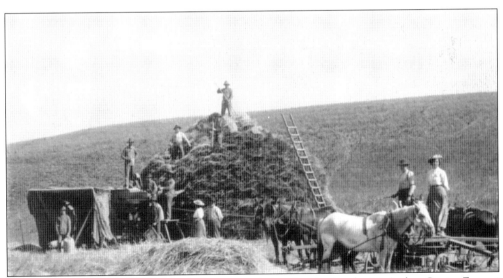

THRESHING, 1904. This photograph shows grain being threshed at the McArther-Coates-Zanoni ranch. Threshing separates the seeds or grain from the straw. The mild climate of La Honda would allow many types of crops to grow, but much of the area is forested or steep. (Courtesy Rob and Kathy [Zanone] Wolf.)

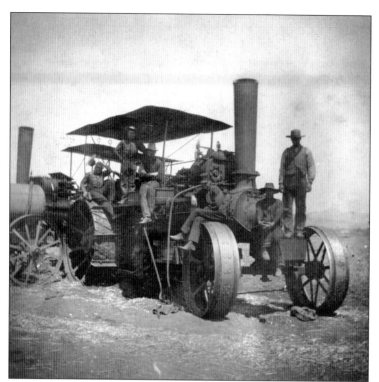

STEAM TRACTOR, c. 1910. This photograph shows a steam-run tractor on the Weeks ranch in La Honda. Just as in transportation, the increased productivity from these motorized vehicles soon replaced animal labor in farming. (Courtesy Redwood City Library.)

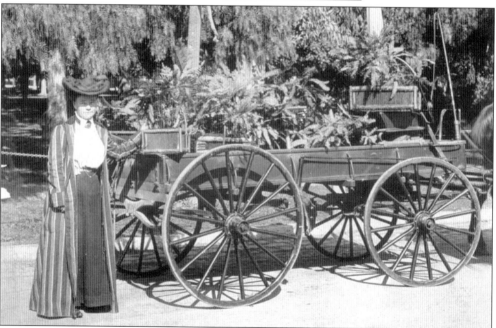

SELLING PLANTS. Ferns, redwood burls, and other plants were collected around the La Honda area to sell in the cities. This arrangement allowed the city-dwellers to obtain a wide variety of plant species while providing income to the local area as the lumber industry was dying. La Honda was also popular as an area to collect edible mushrooms. This photograph of a La Honda fern merchant was taken in San Jose. (Courtesy Redwood City Library.)

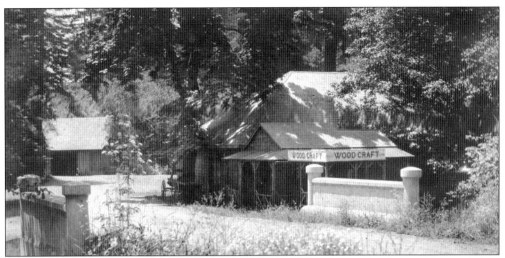

CRAFTS, 1940. The sales of crafts have long provided income to the La Honda area. This craft shop was about a mile east of La Honda. The Woodruff dance hall can be seen behind the woodcraft shop; a bridge over Woodruff creek is in the foreground. (Courtesy Pam McReynolds.)

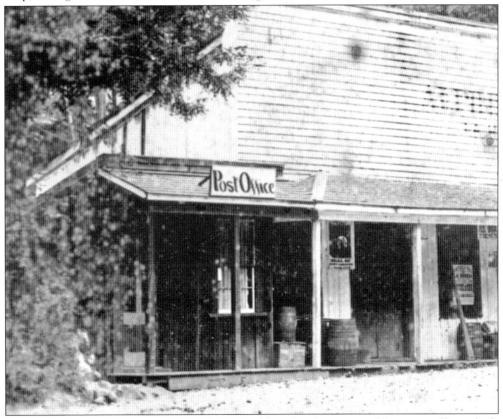

FIRST POST OFFICE, C. 1875. The residents in Old La Honda petitioned for a post office, which was approved and constructed in 1873. However, this post office moved to new La Honda in 1878. The adjacent store was kept open until the owners realized they couldn't compete with the Sears store in new La Honda. (Courtesy Mary and George Bordi.)

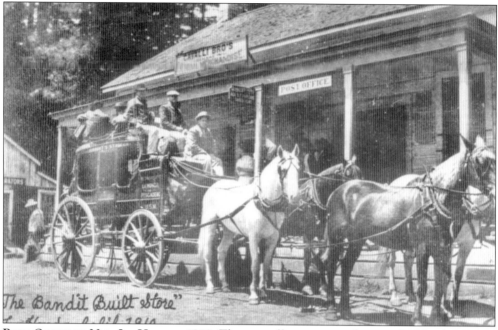

POST OFFICE IN NEW LA HONDA, 1910. The post office was moved to new La Honda in 1878. In 1913, Ida Sears was appointed postmaster. The post office was originally located in the Hotel La Honda but was moved to the Cavalli Brothers store. The stage is marked U.S.M. for United States Mail. (Courtesy Rob and Kathy [Zanone] Wolf.)

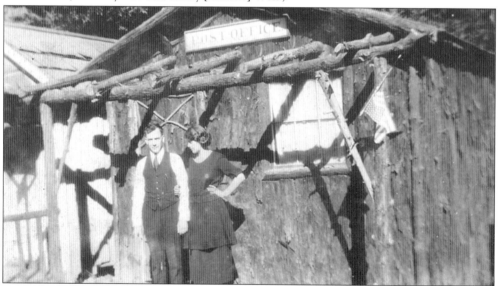

POST OFFICE, C. 1925. This rustic post office is believed to have been located next to the Cavalli store. The flag on the building has 42 stars. This was the unofficial, anticipated flag of 1890. In 1889, the U.S. flag had 38 stars. Before July 4, 1890, when a new flag would take effect, four more states were added to the Union. Forty-two star flags were made in anticipation, but then, on July 3, 1890, Congress admitted Idaho, so the flag should have had 43 stars. But few 43 star flags were created, since seven days later, Wyoming was added as the 44th state. The date of the flag doesn't match the date of the photograph. (Courtesy Charlie Catania.)

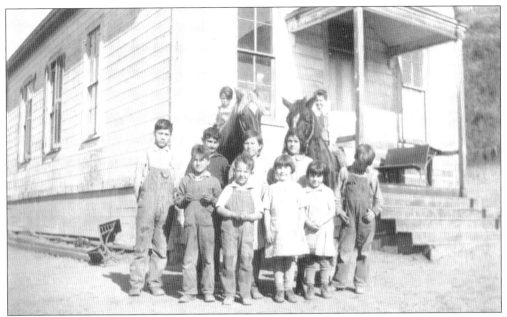

ALPINE SCHOOL, C. 1929. The Alpine Elementary School District was formed in 1874 and was located in the Alpine area of La Honda. An 1882 newspaper request for a teacher there had this unusual stipulation for employment: "She must consent, in order to get the position, to capture one of the bachelor trustees, and to step aside as soon as she has achieved matrimony, that trustee number two may be accommodated." Five of the students in the photograph are siblings from the Bordi family: Ameil, Stella, Arlene, Beatrice, and Gus. Another sibling, George Bordi, who still lives in the area with his wife, Mary, from San Gregorio, started school there the following year. The school closed in 1953 because of insufficient attendance. (Courtesy George and Mary Bordi.)

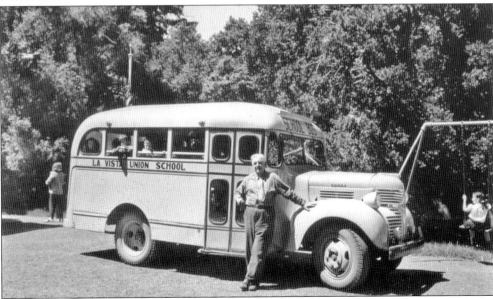

BUSSING TO THE OLD SCHOOLHOUSE, 1949. This photograph shows Matt Zanoni outside the old La Honda schoolhouse, which is now a private residence in Cuesta La Honda. La Vista was the school district at that time. (Courtesy Rob and Kathy [Zanone] Wolf.)

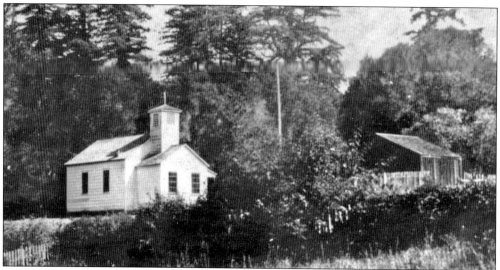

LA HONDA SCHOOL. The La Honda School opened in 1870. Miss Loag was the first teacher. The La Honda School district was created in 1874 but almost immediately closed because of a lack of funds. In 1876, with the help of the La Honda Grange, the school reopened, and Julia Woodhams became the schoolteacher for 34 students. In 1888, the students got the day off when a bear was waiting for them in front of the school. A horse stable for the students is on the right side. (Courtesy Rob and Kathy [Zanone] Wolf.)

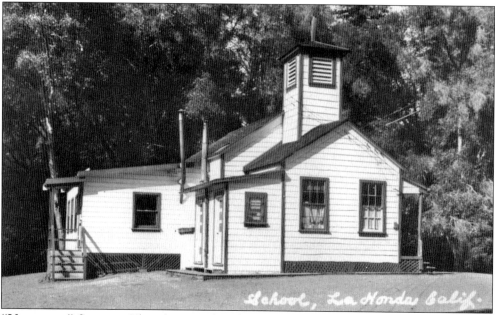

"UPGRADED" SCHOOL. This photograph is different from the previous one because there is now a building extension and two adjacent doors on the left side of the school. These doors are attached bathrooms—one for the boys and another for the girls. Before then, there were only detached, two-hole outhouses for the students—boys on the right side and girls on the left side. The old school was replaced by a new school on Sears Ranch Road in 1953. The schoolhouse was used for awhile in the 1950s as a theater and Odd Fellows lodge, and it is now a private residence. (Courtesy Rob and Kathy [Zanone] Wolf.)

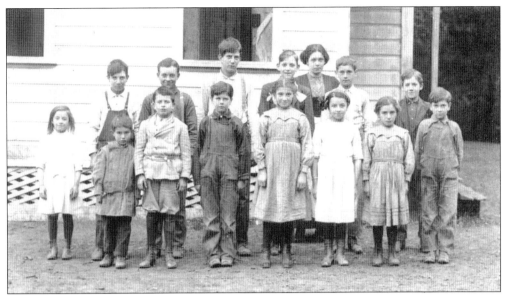

LA HONDA SCHOOL CLASS. This shot was a typical class portrait taken outside a one-room schoolhouse. In 1870, the average attendance was 6 students, which climbed to 19 in 1939. Teachers had to instruct eight grades in a single classroom, and in 1874, some high school students were even enrolled there. Ben Cavalli is shown just to the left of the teacher. (Courtesy Milton Cavalli.)

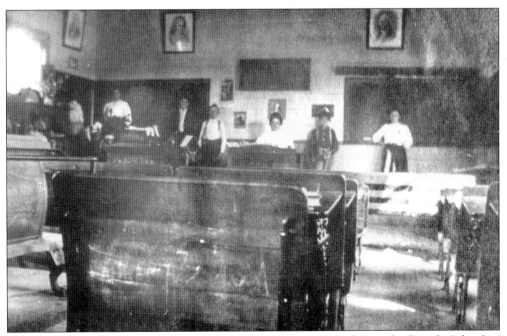

INSIDE THE SCHOOLHOUSE, C. 1902. This photograph is inside the nearby Seaside School in San Gregorio, which is still maintained in a state of "arrested decay" by a private family. The size and appearance of this school is very similar to the inside of the La Honda schoolhouse at the time. Students sometimes had the same teacher for all eight years. (Courtesy Mary and George Bordi.)

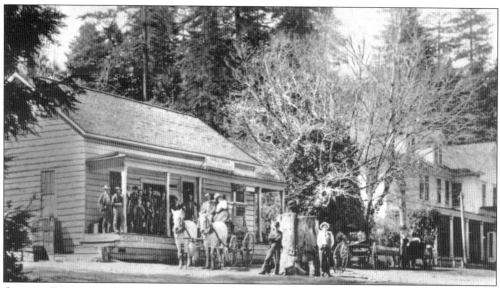

CAVALLI BROTHERS STORE, 1909. The "bandit built" store was bought by Frank Cavalli from the Blomquist brothers in 1903. In October 1879, three dozen eggs cost 75¢, and butter cost 22.5¢ per pound at the store. The store was located at the blackberry patch to the left of the present Pioneer Market. Note the original Hotel La Honda on the right side of the photograph. (Courtesy Rob and Kathy [Zanone] Wolf.)

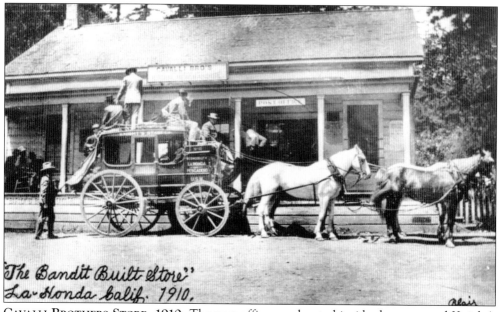

CAVALLI BROTHERS STORE, 1910. The post office was located inside the store, and Knight's stagecoach can be seen delivering the mail outside. Fifty books were sent to the store in 1916 by San Mateo County when it became a new library branch. (Courtesy Turk and Kim Borick.)

C. A. Cavalli
F. G. Cavalli

Cavalli Bros.

General Merchandise

Resident Agents
Queen Insurance Co.
De Laval Separator and Dairy Supply

La Honda, _____ 1918

Account No. _____

Phone:
Redwood City 1711 J3

Sold to A. Bordi

Terms _____

McBride Carbon Copy Bill Ledger   McBride Ledger Mfg. Co., San Francisco

1919

Sep 13/17	Bill renderde	50	91
1918			
May 11	1 Bot Renett	85	
Sep 23	2 can Tomatoes 40 Honey 15 Salt 80 Caches 25 Wine 60	2	20
"	Candy 15 St Tobaco 60	75	
Oct 20	3 Bread 30 yeast 05 Shell 25 2 Socks 100	2	60
Nov 25	Sugar 210 Tobaco 30 1 gal Wine 70 1 Tob 25	3	35
Dec 4	1/4 Flour 345 2 macaroni 140	4	85
5	3 D. 40 1 St Mids 300 1 St Bran 200	5	40
24	1 gal Whiskey 800 Wine 100 Cheese 130	10	30
1919			
March 10	Shoe 650 Sock 100 St Tobaco 75 Peda 25 C Paper 10 Vinega 30	8	90
26	10lb Flour 80 5 tq Tobaco 80 Ey 10 Chocolate 12 cheese 100 peace 15	2	97
"	Sardine 25 Broom 85 coffee 145 yeast 05 Cahes 20	2	70
27	A Clock 130 Caches 20 Beans 100 oil 35 Chocolate 10 Phone 30	3	45
Apr 2	2 Bread 20 L Deering 25 B. ami 10 Leggi 35 V Ey 20	1	10
"	L Ey 20 V Soup 25 Chocolate 15 C Sandwich 20 W Sime 50	1	30
5	Flour 335 Chocolate 35 Tobaco 65	4	35
12	5 gal P oil 75 Bread 10 Overalls 250 Soap 15	1	10
15	25 lb C Feed 125 P H Flour 40 By Overalls Return	1	65
19	Bread 15 Mustard 15 P apple 40 Chocolate 35 W soda 25	1	30
"	1 pkg H W Powder 30 coffee 50 Clams 15	95	
29	Cheese 100 Sugar 50 Bread 40 Caches 20 5 gal P oil 75	2	85
May 10	Cheese 50 F g t 80 Caches 40 Bread 40 Oysters 60 Clams 40	2	90
"	ink 05 Raisins 25 I seed 10 D Meat 15 C Feed 125	1	80
13	P oil 75 1 Caches 30 Soap 10 Bread 54 Tomales 25 P apple 45 P 25	2	65
17	Bread 50 Coffee 145	1	95
24	Caches 20 Candy 25 Salt 25 cheese 100 Beans 50 M yeast 05	2	25
31	5 gal P oil 75 Jello 25 Oysters 30	1	20
		128	98
		2	50

CAVALLI BROTHERS STORE RECEIPT, 1919. This 1918–1919 invoice covers over a year of purchases. A 1904 *Redwood City Democrat* advertisement stated that the Cavalli Brothers store carried "a fine stock of general merchandise, wines, liquors, cigars, everything you want, sold there at city prices." (Courtesy George and Mary Bordi.)

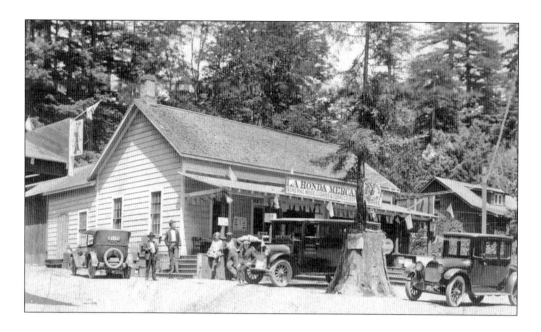

ELECTRICITY AND TELEPHONE SERVICES. A telephone exchange was installed at the store by Pacific Bell Telephone and Telegraph Company in 1923, and electricity came to La Honda in 1924 because of the efforts of the La Honda Improvement Club. Power lines and a Pacific Bell sign on the store in both photographs show that these services had arrived. There is a story that Frank Cavalli threw an apple core into Carter's stump, shown in the top photograph, and an apple tree grew, although the tree in this photograph appears to be a redwood. The above photograph was taken around 1924, and the one below in the snow was taken in 1932. (Above courtesy Charlie Catania; below courtesy Rob and Kathy [Zanone] Wolf.)

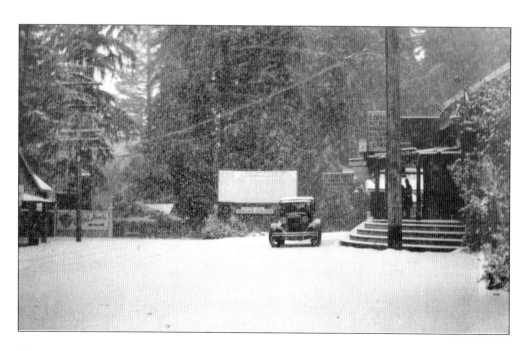

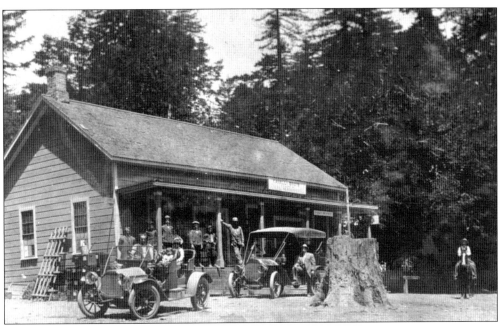

FROM CAVALLI TO LA HONDA MERCANTILE. The top photograph shows the Cavalli Brothers store in 1912. Charles Cavalli was second from the left. The store was sold to R. E. Woodhams, A. Woodhams, and Edgar D. Bartley in 1920, and the name was changed to the La Honda Mercantile Company. George Finley was the next to own the store under this name. The tree stump in front of the store in the top photograph was known as Carter's Stump. It was a 5-foot-wide redwood riddled with bullets and originally used for hitching horses. It was removed in the bottom photograph to increase parking for the store. (Above courtesy Bud Foss; right courtesy Charlie Catania.)

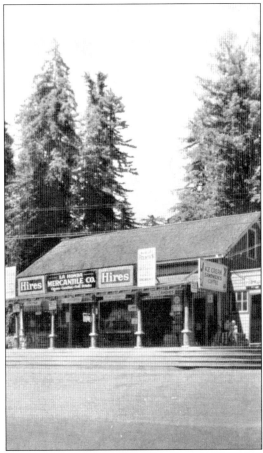

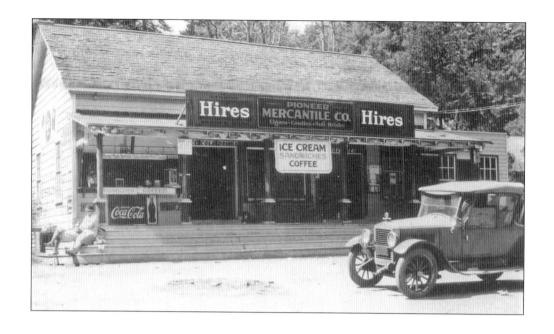

PIONEER MERCANTILE COMPANY. The name of the La Honda Mercantile Company was changed to Pioneer Mercantile Company. In 1939, the La Honda store site became State Historical Landmark No. 343. The store was torn down in 1959, but Mrs. Pete Towne built a model of the old store on a scale of one inch to one foot that was displayed in the San Mateo County courthouse in Redwood City in the 1960s. (Above courtesy Rob and Kathy [Zanone] Wolf; below courtesy Kim and Turk Borick.)

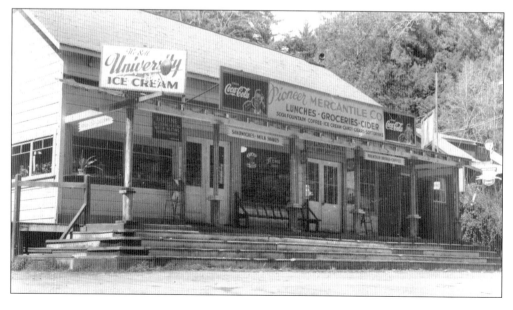

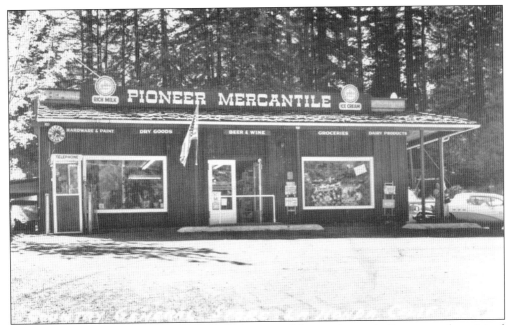

NEW PIONEER MARKET. A new store called Pioneer Mercantile was built next to the original "bandit built" store, and the old store was torn down in 1959. The store shown in the photograph is the one called Pioneer Market that remains there today. (Courtesy Turk and Kim Borick.)

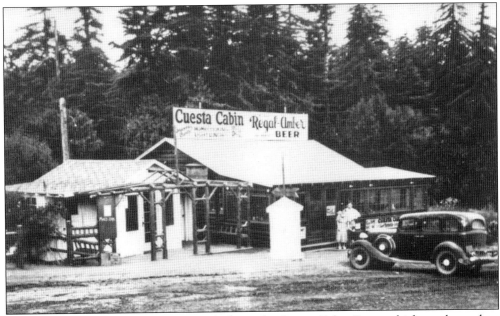

CUESTA CABIN STORE. This photograph shows the Cuesta Cabin Store, which was located on Entrada in the Cuesta area of La Honda. The store was operated by John and Gen Harrington and burned down in the 1950s. (Courtesy Charlie Catania.)

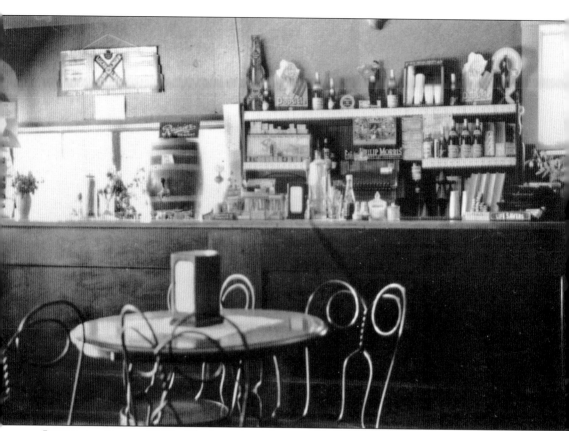

INSIDE THE STORE, 1940s. The bar side of the mercantile store was turned into a soda fountain in the 1940s, although it still served beer. The right side of the store sold groceries (Courtesy Rob and Kathy [Zanone] Wolf.)

Six

TRANSPORTATION

There was no fast or easy way around or over the Santa Cruz Mountains near early La Honda. A large section of the coast-side territory was physically isolated from the rest of the peninsula, only reachable by horseback. The physical isolation made it difficult to get crops and dairy products from La Honda to the bay side and San Francisco and to get supplies into La Honda; this slowed the social and economic growth of the area.

Two early, private enterprises connected the east side of the Santa Cruz Mountains with the coast side: the Redwood City–San Gregorio Turnpike in 1868, and the Searsville–La Honda Turnpike in 1874–1878. Until 1868, present-day Woodside was the western end of Knight's Stage. But by 1872, Simon "Sime" Knight had established a regular service to San Gregorio and Pescadero. The stage roads brought tourists to fish, hunt, camp, and enjoy the beaches and forests.

The Searsville–La Honda Turnpike Company followed what is now Old La Honda Road and reached La Honda in 1876. This turnpike ran through beautiful redwood groves and was a popular route to the coast. Passengers had to get off the stage and walk up the steepest parts of the route. The road was covered in gravel from the Red Barn at the Weeks ranch to La Honda Junction. Robinson J. Weeks had the contract to construct the road, which cut through his ranch.

In 1896, Knight died, and his coach business went to his son, Walter. But privately owned automobiles, a decline in popularity of the coast, and the Ocean Shore Railroad put Knight's Stage Company out of business in 1910. Between the years 1907 and 1920, the Ocean Shore Railroad left San Francisco at 8:10 a.m., and passengers arrived in San Gregorio at 10:45 a.m., where passengers could continue on to La Honda. By 1920, cars and trucks on improved roads also put the Ocean Shore Railroad out of business.

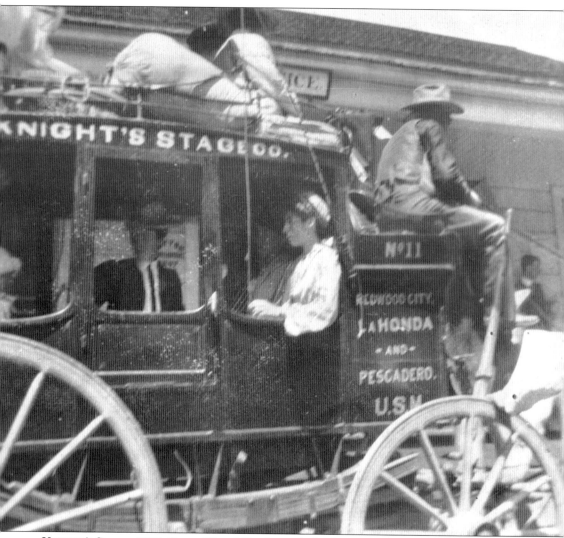

Knight's Stage, 1897. Simon "Sime" Knight made the first stage trip to La Honda in 1872 when the Redwood City–Pescadero Road opened. Knight used a six-horse team during the summer and a two- or four-horse team during the off-season. The stages in 1873 could fit 18 passengers and a driver. In 1877, the fare from Redwood City to La Honda was $1.75, and the trip took about six hours. Knight was also the Wells Fargo and U.S. mail agent. Sime Knight had carried U.S. mail almost free for years, "maybe a dinner or two was his compensation," according to a Redwood City newspaper, but Knight put in a bid to deliver mail and was awarded the contract. Before motorized vehicles, summer business was good for Knight between the La Honda campsites and the filled hotels. (Courtesy Bud Foss.)

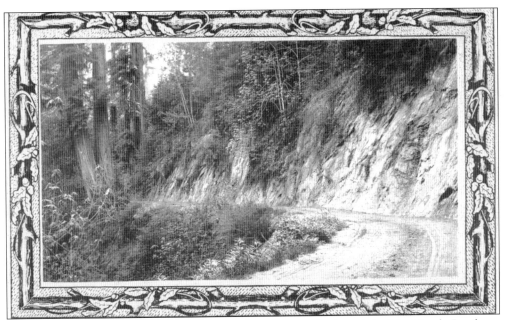

OLD LA HONDA ROAD, 1910. As shown in this photograph, the original La Honda Road was bare dirt. This almost guaranteed that the ride was rough, the trip was long, and that the road was impassable because of mud during parts of the winter. In 1903, Knight's Stage Company advertised in the *Redwood City Democrat*, "Easy roads" and "comfortable coaches"—terms that would almost certainly not meet today's standards. (Courtesy Rob and Kathy [Zanone] Wolf.)

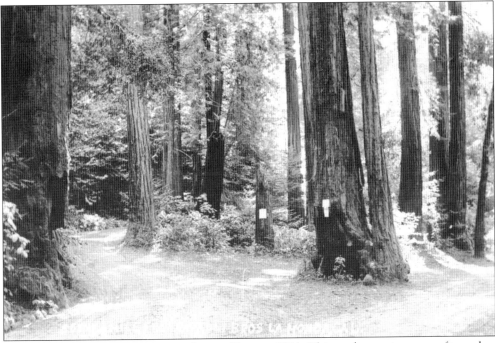

INTERSECTION OF LA HONDA AND ALPINE ROADS, 1911. This road scene just west of town has changed considerably since the time of this photograph. This intersection appears to have been not much more than a poorly marked path in 1911. (Courtesy Milton Cavalli.)

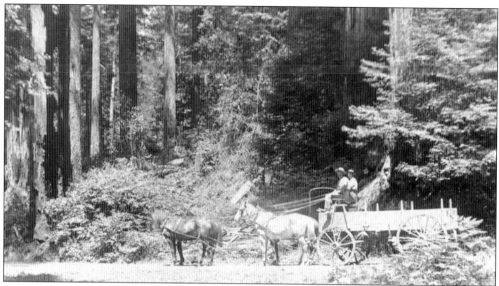

FREIGHT TEAM, 1884. This photograph shows a typical freight team on La Honda Road. These wagons were designed more for carrying freight than passengers, unlike the stages that could comfortably carry both. (Courtesy Bud Foss.)

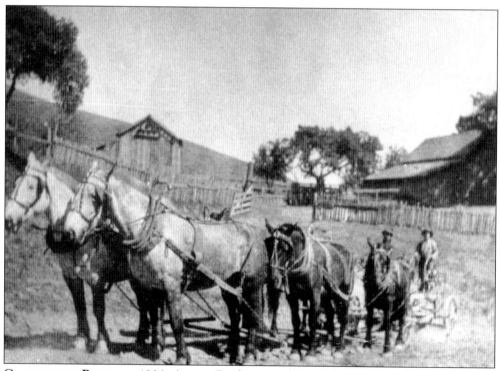

GRADING THE ROADS, C. 1920. Antone Bordi manned the grader, and Peter O'Hara drove the team when they graded roads in the La Honda Alpine area. This area is now part of Portola State Park. Without frequent grading, the roads developed ruts during the rains and were impassable. (Courtesy George and Mary Bordi.)

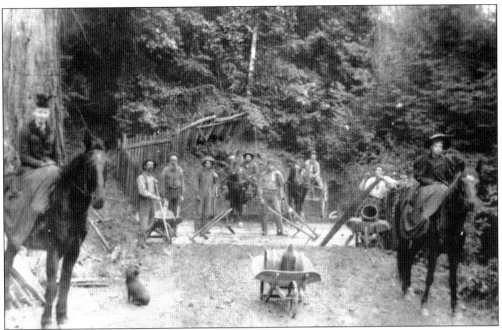

BUILDING A BRIDGE, 1896. The photograph shows a bridge being built across a creek using only hand tools. Pictured from left to right are Susy Murphy (on horse), Ellis Davis, Moses Murphy, Ben Rodgers Jr., Jack Albee, Ed Lasswell, Westly Reynolds, Joe Felix, and Ceres Rodgers (on horse). (Courtesy Bud Foss.)

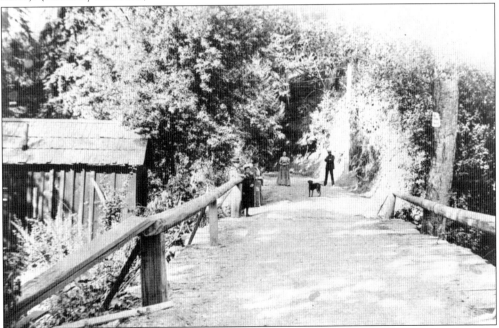

BRIDGE ACROSS WOODRUFF CREEK, 1895. The finished bridge, resulting from the work in the top photograph, might have looked like this one crossing Woodruff Creek. Tillie Steinberg and Newton Ray are standing in the road. Tillie's mother, Mary, was bitten by a tarantula in La Honda in 1887, which was said to have nearly killed her. (Courtesy Bud Foss.)

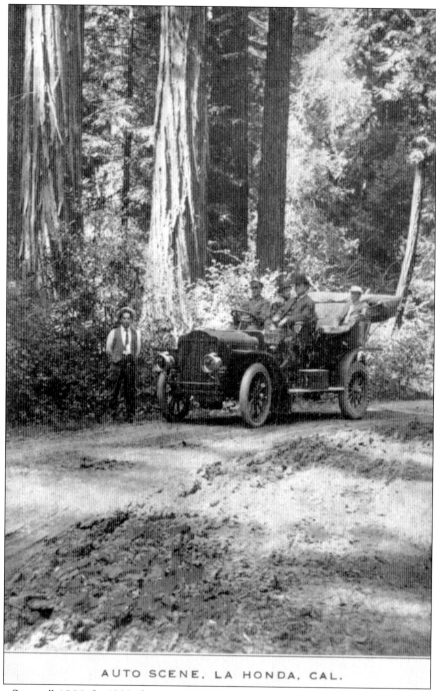

AUTO SCENE, LA HONDA, CAL.

"AUTO SCENE," 1909. In 1909, the same year as this photograph, Dempsey's Automobile Book for California said this about traveling to La Honda: "Before motor cars set time and distance at defiance . . . it was a matter of days and involved a long, tiresome stage ride over the summit which robbed the traveler of his power to enjoy the magnificent views. . . . That is all changed with the coming of the gasoline age and La Honda, the odd, picturesque village that lies at the bottom of those hills." (Courtesy Karen Delee.)

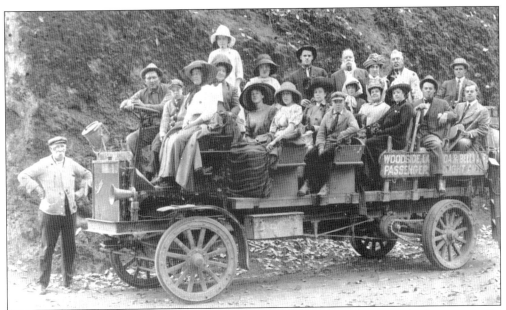

Wetherbee's Motor Stage, 1915. In 1905, Al Wetherbee started a motor-truck service to La Honda. In 1912, he purchased a Gramm motor truck that could carry 22 passengers, a driver, and freight. This was the beginning of the quick end to stage service to La Honda, which stopped in 1906. The side of the vehicle reads, "Woodside, La Honda, and Bellvale Passenger and Freight Auto." The truck doesn't have pneumatic tires, which must have made for a rough and tiresome ride over the mountains. Al Wetherbee is in the driver's seat. (Courtesy Bud Foss.)

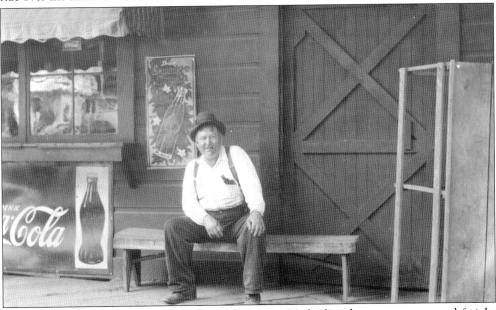

Al Wetherbee in Front of Old Mill, c. 1930. Wetherbee drove passengers and freight over the hill to La Honda. Wetherbee once drove a 20-mule team for the Borax Company in the desert and afterward drove a 4-team wagon in the Santa Cruz Mountains. He would take orders from any rancher or woodcutter he saw along the way and was known for keeping all the details in his head. (Courtesy Milton Cavalli.)

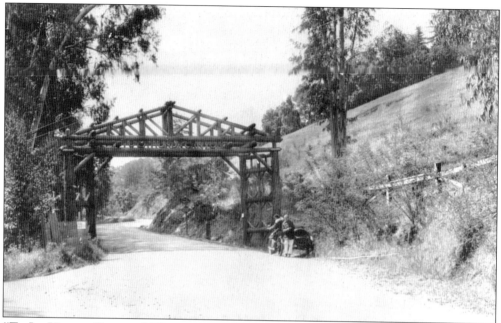

"To La Honda Canyon." This entrance displaying the words "To La Honda Canyon" faced west on Highway 84 near Woodside. Portola Road intersects Highway 84 from the left of the photograph, making a hairpin turn. (Courtesy Rob and Kathy [Zanone] Wolf.)

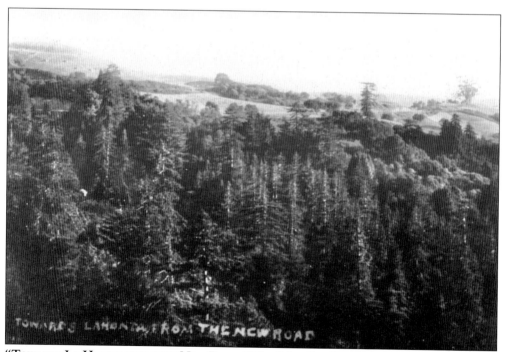

"Towards La Honda from the New Road." The "New Road" is the current La Honda Road, also known as Highway 84. It is wider and less windy than the previous road over the summit, which is now called Old La Honda Road. (Courtesy Rob and Kathy [Zanone] Wolf.)

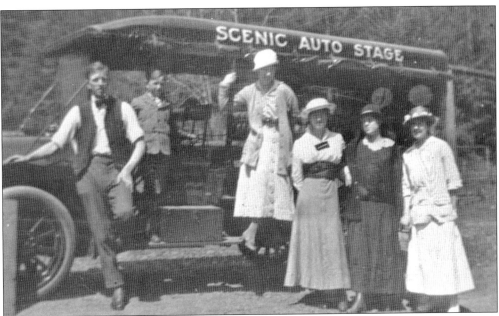

SCENIC AUTO STAGE. In 1915, Al Wetherbee discontinued his motor-truck service, and that same year Edgar Woodhams started his "Scenic Auto Stage" from Redwood City to La Honda. The Overland bus was driven by either Edgar or his son Archie. The vehicle was also used to haul freight and, in 1918, mail after taking over the delivery from the Ocean Shore Railroad. Summer business was good, though service was not continuous in the slower winter months. Woodhams sold his business to George Carr in 1926. The photograph shows Archie Woodhams and his son Bud and passengers in Woodhams's "Scenic Auto Stage." (Courtesy Bud Foss.)

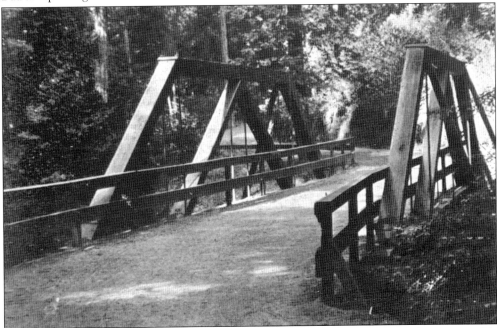

BRIDGE AT LA HONDA, C. 1916. By 1916, bridges like this one were substantial structures able to support modern motor vehicles. (Courtesy Bud Foss.)

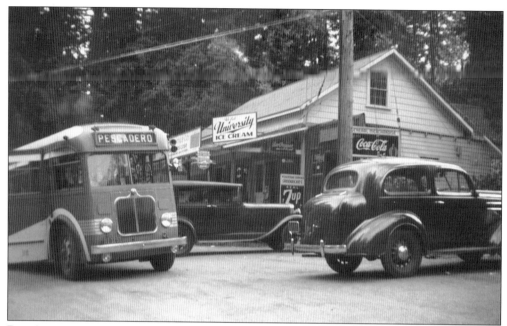

Bus Service, 1940. The Peninsula Rapid Transit Company ran buses to La Honda but was supplanted by Greyhound Lines in 1929. The first vehicles were 21-passenger buses known as "bathtubs." The time and price to go from Redwood City to La Honda decreased greatly over the years. In 1877, it took about six hours and cost $1.75 one way by stage. By 1940, it took 45 minutes and cost 35¢ to go this distance by bus. This photograph shows a Greyhound bus in 1940 parked in front of the Pioneer Mercantile market. (Courtesy Bud Foss.)

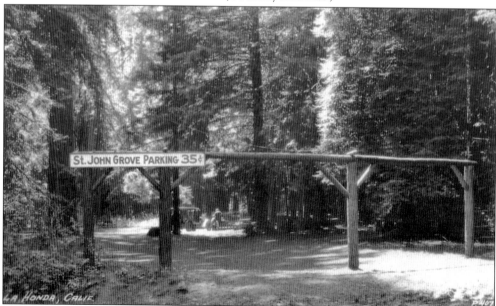

St. John Grove Parking, c. 1948. This parking area was located across from where the windmill now stands. The area also included a picnic and camping area. It was used for parking for La Honda Bandit Day in the late 1940s. St. John was the last name of a La Honda resident. (Courtesy Rob and Kathy [Zanone] Wolf.)

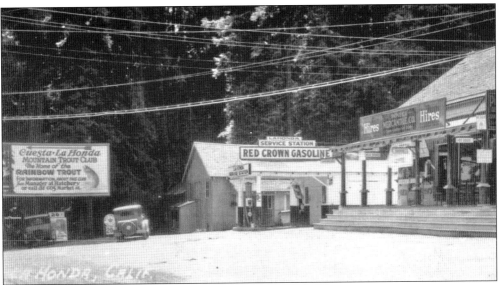

RED CROWN SERVICE STATION, C. 1930. A series of service stations came and went in La Honda. A billboard on the left side of the photograph advertises Cuesta La Honda as "Home of the Rainbow Trout." Cuesta La Honda had its own fish hatchery at that time. It appears that gasoline then was 20¢ per gallon. Today La Honda does not have a gas station. (Courtesy Rob and Kathy [Zanone] Wolf.)

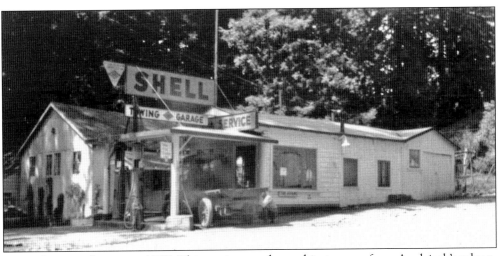

SHELL SERVICE STATION, 1937. This station was located just across from Applejack's saloon. Service stations in town included a Red Crown station in the early 1930s, a Standard Oil by 1932, a Veltex station in the 1940s, and a Signal station in the 1950s. Most of these service stations stood near where Edgar Woodhams and Edgar Bartley had a dance hall in the 1920s. (Courtesy Rob and Kathy [Zanone] Wolf.)

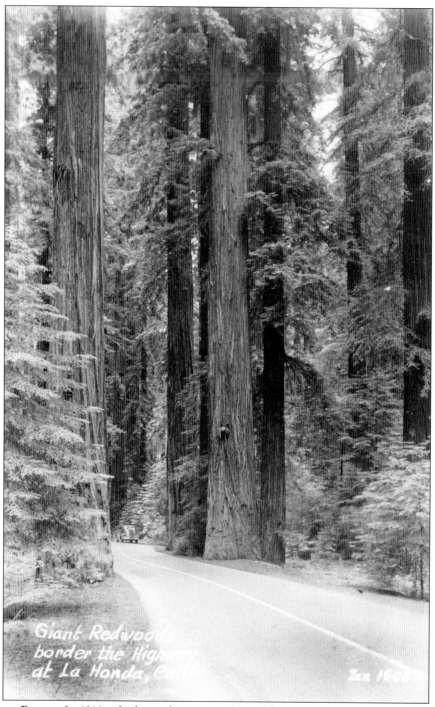

Giant Redwoods border the Highway at La Honda, Calif.

MODERN ROADS. In 1916, a highway district was formed by San Francisco, San Mateo, Santa Clara, and Santa Cruz Counties to build Skyline Boulevard, which was the first cross-county road in California. By 1923, the State Highway Commission had finished the 30 miles of Skyline Boulevard between San Francisco and La Honda Road. The photograph shows the road to La Honda. (Courtesy Charlie Catania.)

Seven

MOUNTAIN RETREAT

The following description of La Honda campers appeared in the *San Francisco Argonaut* on August 30, 1879, "On the Fourth of July evening, La Honda had its open-air dance. The platform was built under the trees opposite the hotel, and hundreds of people had come miles to jostle each other about to the music of two squeaking fiddles. All day long dust-covered wagons had been bringing in their human loads; country girls, with their fresh cheerful faces, and bright simple dresses. . . . The campers had turned out in full force to look on at the unusual scene, made weird and unearthly by the lurid light of the bonfires glancing against the somber shadows of the trees, and almost putting out the dull steady glow of the Chinese lanterns with their chrysalis shape and butterfly color."

Besides campers, La Honda drew fishermen and hunters. Hunting included deer, quail, rabbit, and sometimes squirrel. An amusing quote about squirrel hunting comes from a 1916 book titled *Founding of Spanish California,* by Charles E. Chapman, "The grey squirrel is no longer considered game in San Mateo County. They are worth more alive from an aesthetic point of view to satisfy the outer man, than they are dead to satisfy the inner man."

Many lodges were built, especially in the 1920s, to accommodate those who wanted to enjoy the natural beauty of the area without camping. La Honda was the place where many Bay Area residents, especially San Franciscans, went for relaxation, although its popularity waned as other recreation areas became more accessible. Today few people come to La Honda as campers, and all of the elegant lodges are gone, mostly as a result of fires.

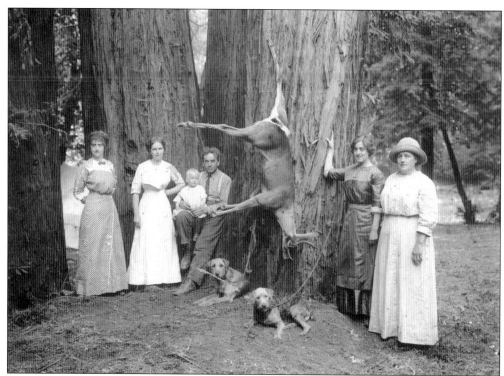

HUNTING. After the logging boom, La Honda functioned as a mountain retreat, drawing city-weary San Franciscans who wanted to relax, camp, fish, and hunt. Hunting included deer, quail, and rabbit. The below photograph includes Louie Zanoni (second from left) and Charlie Wyman (third from left). (Above courtesy Milton Cavalli; below courtesy Rob and Kathy [Zanone] Wolf.)

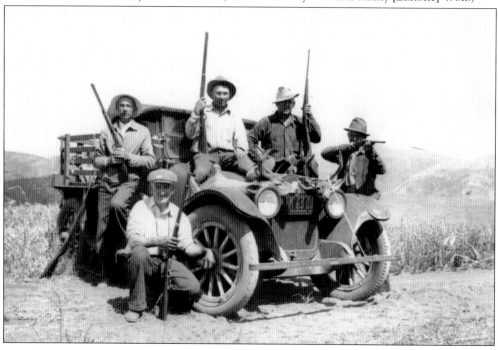

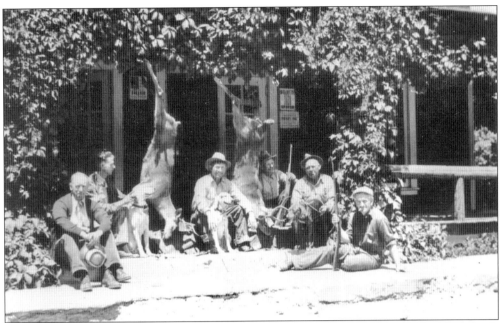

HUNTING, 1925. This hunting scene shows Frank Cavalli on the left, Charlie Wyman (with the dog), and Louie Zanoni on the far right outside Bonzani's Lodge after a successful deer hunt. (Courtesy Rob and Kathy [Zanone] Wolf.)

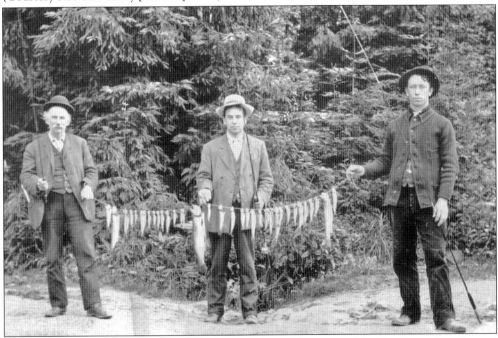

FISHING AFTERMATH. This photograph shows what may be a typical La Honda catch at the end of the day. Fish included trout, steelhead salmon, and stickleback fish. In 1906, the *Redwood City Times-Gazette* reported that "E. J. Crane, far famed as an angler, secured a string of 40 trout near La Honda last Sunday." The photograph shows, from left to right, ? Hause, Charlie Cavalli, and Frank Cavalli. (Courtesy Milton Cavalli.)

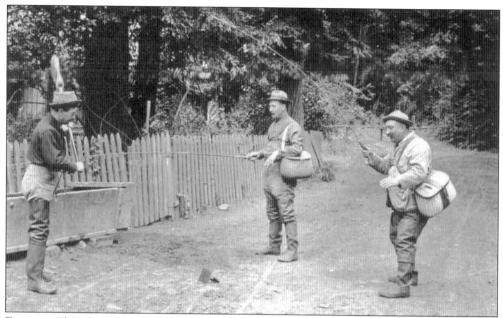

FISHING. This photograph was previously titled "Three Frenchmen," as the subjects' names are not known. They seemed to be playing because the fisherman on the left has a broom in his hand, and the one on the right has a curry comb on the end of his line. The horse trough on the left side of the photograph was a common sight at the time. (Courtesy Rob and Kathy [Zanone] Wolf.)

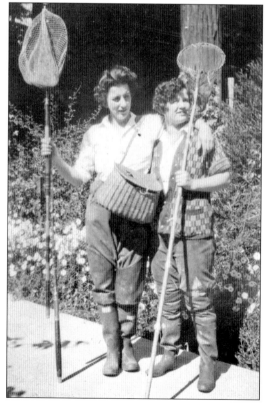

CRAWDAD FISHING, C. 1927. Campers would put a piece of meat on the end of a pole, and when the crawdads grabbed on to eat it, the campers would slip a net under them that the crawdads would fall into. Besides crawdads and fish, campers also sometimes caught and ate frogs. The photograph shows Mary Cavalli (left) and Ruth Sloan getting ready to hunt for crawdads. (Courtesy Milton Cavalli.)

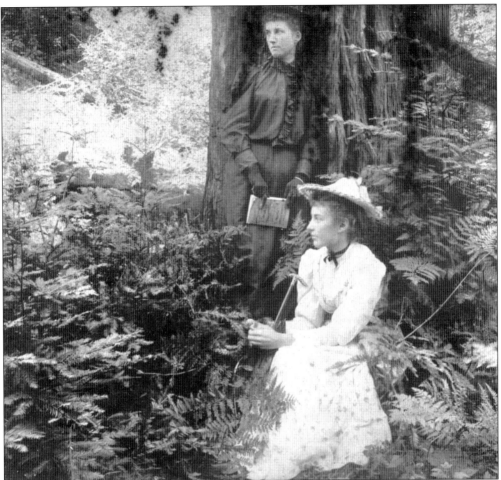

SUMMER CAMPERS, 1888. This photograph of two summer campers shows the abundance of ferns around La Honda in 1888. Non-native plants, like English ivy, have been introduced to the area and are competing with the ferns and other native species. A close-up of the back of the magazine that the standing woman is holding is an 1888 advertisement for Colgate Cashmere Bouquet used for perfuming handkerchiefs. (Courtesy Charlie Catania.)

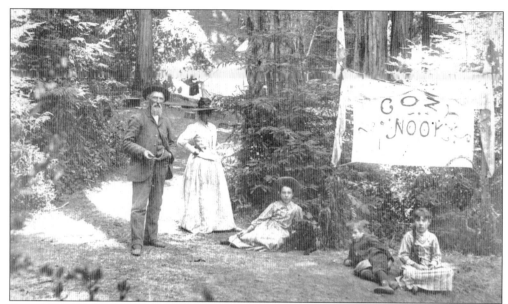

COZY NOOK CAMP. In 1880, the families of Hause and Kessling from San Francisco bought land about a mile from La Honda to camp and fish, putting up a sign on the entrance to the camp the following year that said, "Pioneer Camp, 1881." In 1888, the Oriel camp was set up next to the Pioneer Camp. And in 1891, several other camps opened nearby, including Camp Laurel, Maplewood Camp, Jonah Camp, Brightwood Camp, Tanglewood Camp, Idlewild, Old Camp Mill, Home Sweet Home Camp, Camp Frisco, Camp Polliwog, Peek-a-Boo Camp, and Cozy Nook Camp. (Courtesy Charlie Catania.)

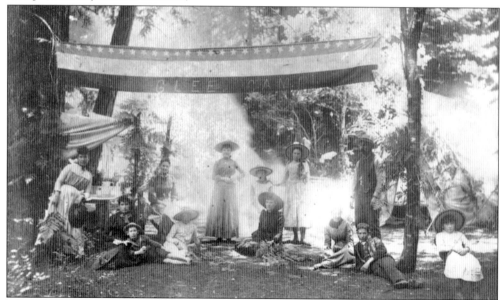

GLEE CAMP. For those campers who didn't want to bring their own camping gear, they could rent it in La Honda. A 1904 *Redwood City Democrat* advertisement said, "Don't take your supplies when going to La Honda for camping. You can get what you want and at moderate prices at Cavalli Brothers in La Honda." Many campgrounds had their own music platforms, and dinners often featured fresh trout. (Courtesy Charlie Catania.)

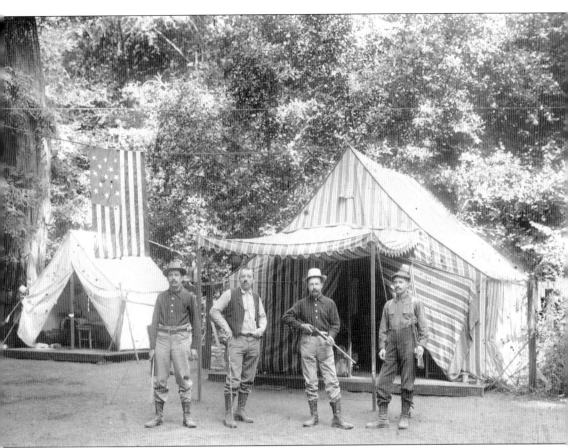

BOHEMIAN CLUB. The members of the exclusive Bohemian Club used to camp at various locations in the redwoods, including Muir Woods, Samuel P. Taylor State Park, and La Honda. The Bohemian Club campsite in La Honda was located across the road from the windmill. In 1899, members started to regularly meet at the Bohemian Grove in Monte Rio, California, near the Russian River. (Courtesy Milton Cavalli.)

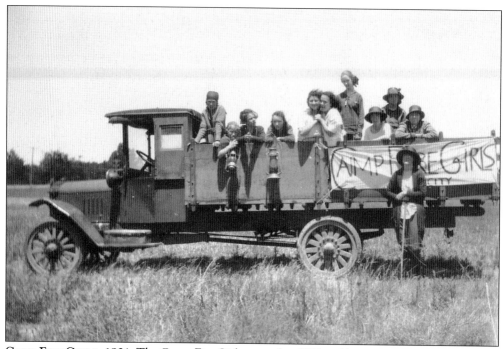

CAMP FIRE GIRLS, 1921. The Camp Fire Girls started in 1910 and became campers in La Honda shortly thereafter. In 1975, The Camp Fire Girls went coed and renamed themselves Camp Fire Boys and Girls. In 2001, they changed their name to Camp Fire USA. (Courtesy Charlie Catania.)

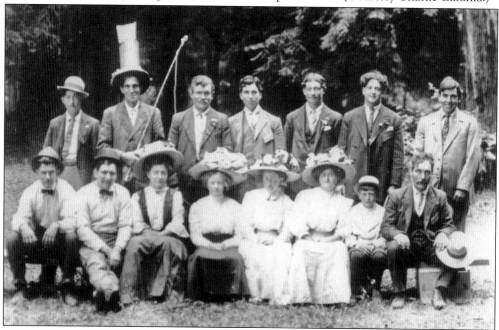

DESTINATION FOR SPECIAL OCCASIONS. From their dress, it appears that the members in this group came to La Honda for a special occasion, such as a wedding. The man in the back row with a stovepipe hat and fishing pole does not seem to be taking the event as seriously as the rest of the group. (Courtesy Rob and Kathy [Zanone] Wolf.)

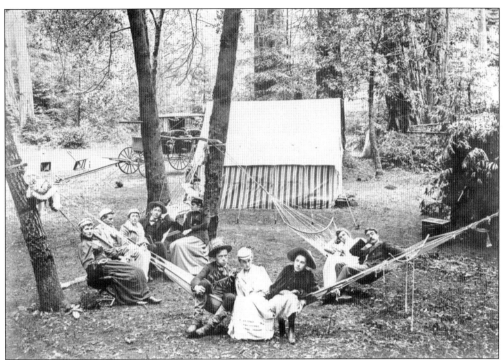

OTHER SUMMER CAMPERS. Nellie McGraw Hedgpeth wrote in her story, "To Pescadero by Stagecoach in 1888," that "the woods around were filled with campers. The camps looked festive with their strings of Japanese lanterns and flags and banners. They seemed to try to outdo each other, and each had a large white cloth sign stretched above the entrance bearing the name of the camp. The names all looked gay and inviting. These campers drove in with all their equipment in a spring wagon and all seemed to have plenty of children. They lived out of doors all summer, and used their tents only to sleep in. There would be gay blankets airing on the lines, or occasionally a wash, or a beautiful bunch of tiger lilies decorating a dinner table, or maybe a bunch of ferns." The above photograph is a Redwood City recreation group in La Honda. (Above courtesy Redwood City Library; below courtesy Charlie Catania.)

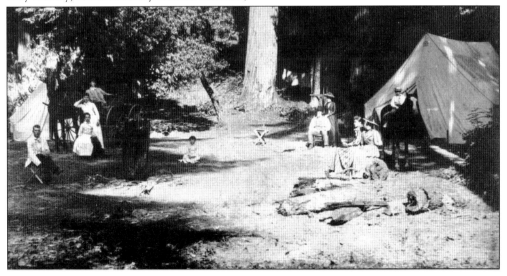

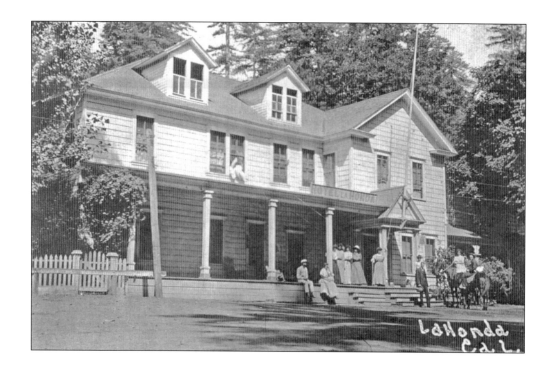

HOTEL LA HONDA, 1878. In 1878, John Sears built the Hotel La Honda. On the main floor was a feed and general store and a post office. The hotel charged $2 per night. In 1903, it was purchased by Frank and Charles Cavalli, who had frog-shooting contests and featured music by Al Cox and his famous Tapioca Band. (Above courtesy Rob and Kathy [Zanone] Wolf; below courtesy Hayden Coggins.)

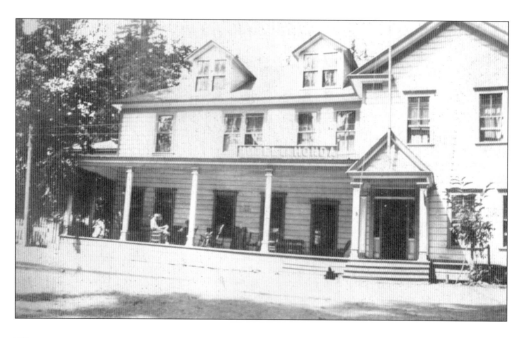

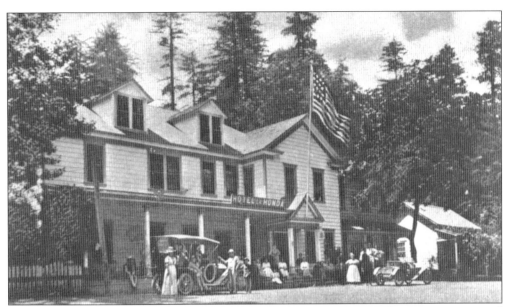

HOTEL LA HONDA, 1912. Campgrounds, consisting of tent platforms and cottages, were owned and maintained by Ida and Annie Sears next to and across from the hotel. A Catholic priest came from Half Moon Bay who would say mass at the Sears campgrounds each Sunday. After a 1914 fire destroyed the hotel, the *Redwood City Democrat* reported, "It was feared that the store of the Cavalli Brothers would also be destroyed, but luckily there was no wind, which fact and the efforts of a bucket brigade saved the property." (Courtesy Bud Foss.)

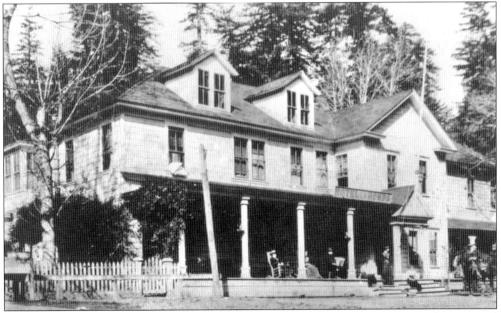

HOTEL LA HONDA, 1878. The *Oakland Tribune* said that for Christmas, "Mrs. Ida Sears and Miss Annie Sears served their guests a big turkey with cranberry sauce, cream of celery soup, plum pudding, and many other things that accompany a royal meal. After dinner the La Honda orchestra (Mrs. Sears, Leonard Sears and Percy St. John) delighted the company with a fine concert." (Courtesy Charlie Catania.)

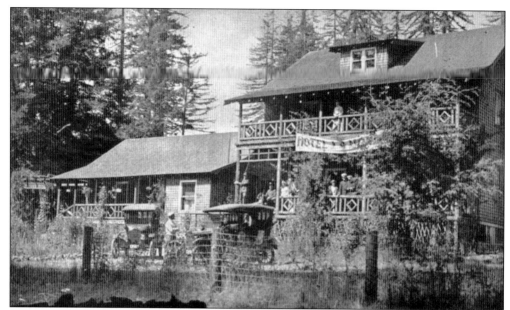

THE NEW HOTEL LA HONDA. After the original La Honda Hotel was destroyed by fire in 1914, John Sears's daughters, Ida and Annie, rebuilt another three-story hotel with the insurance money. (Courtesy Charlie Catania.)

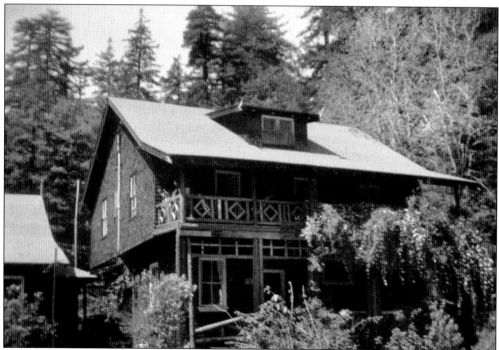

"DOG SAVES LA HONDA," 1949. Like the original Hotel La Honda, this one also perished in a fire. The November 15, 1949, *San Mateo Times* newspaper headlines read, "Dog Saves La Honda as Fire Razes Hotel." The article said, "A springer spaniel named 'Lady' was credited with giving the alarm which saved most of the business district of this community." The dog woke its owner, Lawrence Blomquist, who alerted the rest of the community. (Courtesy Bud Foss.)

LOST LODGES, 1912. Very little is known about some of the resorts that sprang up near La Honda, such as the Flornell Lodge (shown). La Honda was a popular location for campers, hunters, and fisherman, but some of these resorts did not survive into the Depression. (Courtesy Charlie Catania.)

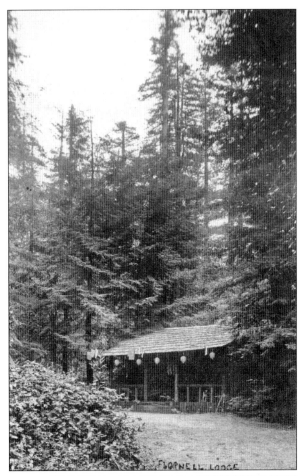

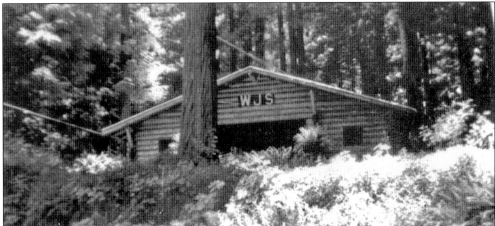

WOODWARDIA LODGE. This log cabin was built in the 1880s by William J. Sullivan, which accounts for the initials on its front. His son was Dan Sullivan, and the Woodwardia Lodge had an area across the road for campers called Sullivan's campground. The cabin was abandoned for many years but is now a private residence. Woodwardia is also a genus of ferns, called chain ferns, which are found in the Northern Hemisphere. (Courtesy Milton Cavalli.)

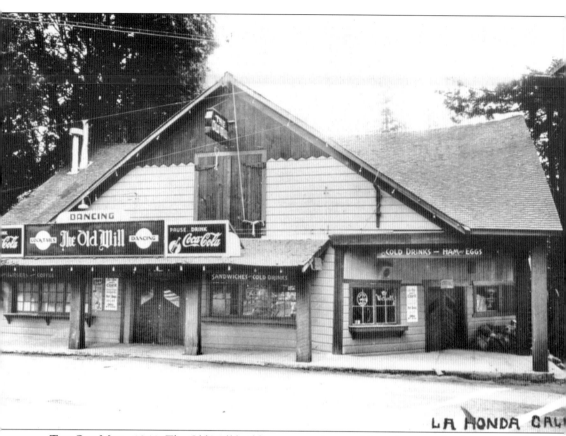

THE OLD MILL, 1940. The Old Mill building was used as a stable and storage for the stagecoaches before 1910. It was originally called the Old Cider Mill when Applejack Gabrielle ran it. The Old Mill was burned down by Howard Sonnickson in 1960 for $10,000 in insurance money. Sonnickson also owned Hoby Choby sandwich and burger shop, located on the left side of the Old Mill. (Courtesy Rob and Kathy [Zanone] Wolf.)

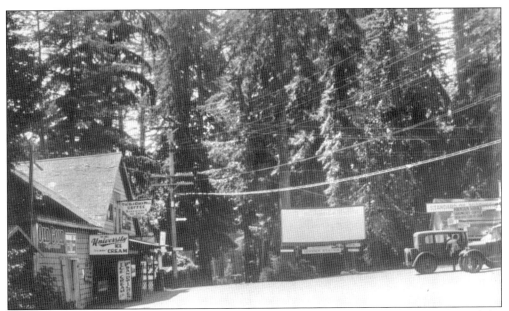

OLD CIDER MILL, 1932. Applejack Gabrielle, who owned Applejack's saloon, also owned the Old Cider Mill and had an apple orchard just behind Kleinsorg's Inn, whose apples he used to make cider. Applejack was also said to be the town bootlegger during Prohibition. Nothing now stands where the Old Cider Mill once stood, which was on the corner just east of Applejack's saloon. (Courtesy Rob and Kathy [Zanone] Wolf.)

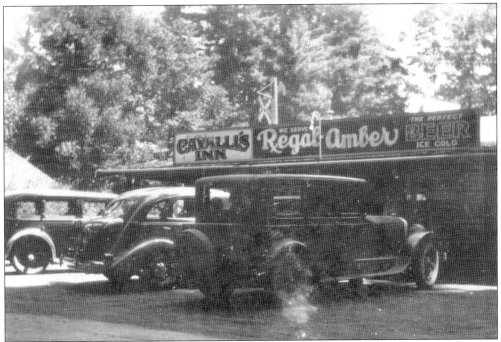

CAVALLI'S INN, C. 1925. Frank Cavalli opened Cavalli's Inn, 200 yards from the "bandit built" store. Cavalli's Inn had a bar, and sandwiches were made there. The inn was later turned into a private residence. (Courtesy Kareen Lindstrom.)

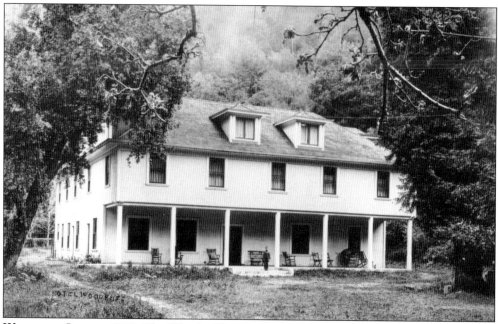

WOODRUFF INN, C. 1910. The Woodruff Inn was a three-story structure built in 1910 by Bert Weeks at the site of the Woodruff Mill, located at the intersection of Woodruff and La Honda Creeks. It boasted 30 rooms. Campers could also stay nearby. (Courtesy Milton Cavalli.)

GOOD EATS   REASONABLE PRICES

A la Carte Service at All Hours
Special Attention to Week-end Parties

WOODRUFF INN
MODERN
...UNDER NEW MANAGEMENT...

LA HONDA ROAD   STAGE FROM REDWOOD CITY
BETWEEN   PASSES DOOR
WOODSIDE AND LA HONDA   PHONE REDWOOD 1711 F 1-2
(OVER)

WOODRUFF INN BUSINESS CARD. Dating of this card might seem difficult since it mentions both the stagecoach, which stopped running in 1910, and the telephone, which did not arrive until 1923. In reality, the later date would be a more accurate one, since the term "stage" was used for the auto stage for years after the horse-drawn variety was gone. (Courtesy Bud Foss.)

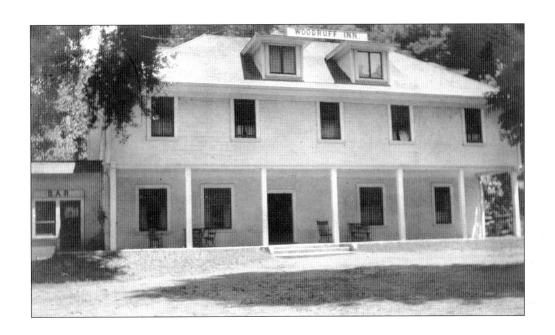

WOODRUFF INN, C. 1920. Bert Weeks's son Percy built a saloon attached to the inn and ran it until World War I. The photograph below shows the inn when it was rented to a Mr. Sheehan. The additional structure on its side is the saloon. In 1918, a new proprietor, Henri A. Devere, had his grand opening of the Woodruff Inn, offering a French dinner and a jazz orchestra until 2:00 a.m. for $2. In 1923, the Woodruff Inn burned to the ground. The nearby cottages and dance hall remained open for while, but eventually they too closed. (Above courtesy Bud Foss; below courtesy Hayden Coggins.)

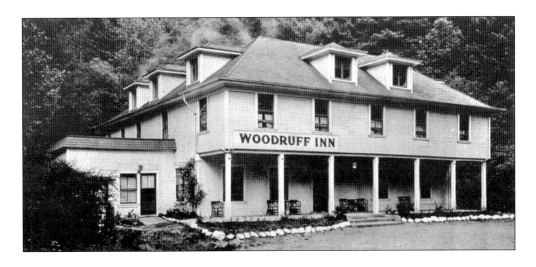

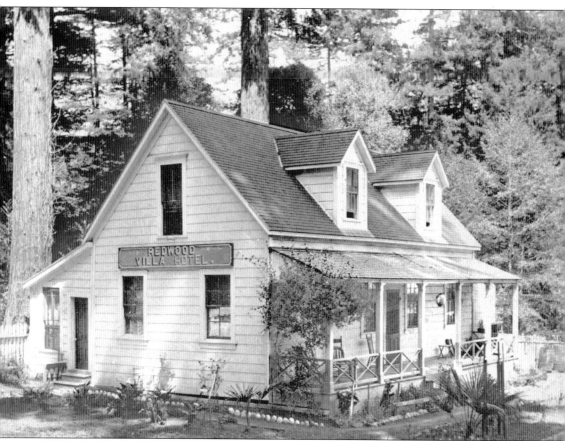

ACKERMAN REDWOOD VILLA HOTEL, C. 1908. August L. Ackerman worked as a blacksmith in town, while his wife ran the hotel. In 1898, he purchased the Catholic church that had been built by Fr. Patrick Riordan from Menlo Park parish and dedicated by Archbishop J. S. Alemany in 1883. Ackerman added a side wing, front porch, and additional rooms to make it into a two-story hotel and saloon. Frank Cavalli purchased the hotel and blacksmith shop after the stage stopped running in 1910 and lived in it with his family. In 1902, an advertisement for the hotel proclaimed, "First class home cooking and plenty of fresh eggs and cream. Rates $8.00 per week." The inn was destroyed by fire in 1909. Tragically, August Ackerman shot and killed both his wife and himself in 1914. (Courtesy Bud Foss.)

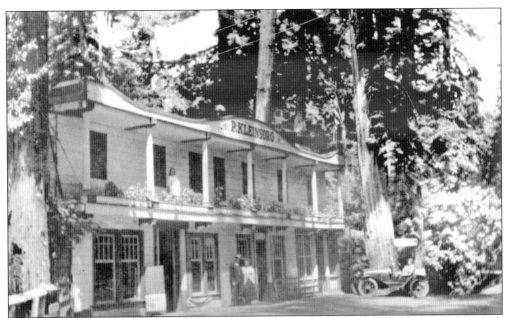

P. KLEINSORG INN, C. 1920. Kleinsorg Inn had a soda fountain and sandwich shop on the left side, a dance hall on the right side, and a bowling alley below the main level. The inn also had picnic grounds and allowed camping. A reference to the owner was found in the 1921 *Redwood City Standard* and reads, "When he refused to get off the La Honda road, which has been closed for some time undergoing repairs, Peter Kleinsorg, proprietor of Kleinsorg's resort at La Honda, was arrested . . . and charged with disturbing the peace." (Courtesy Charlie Catania.)

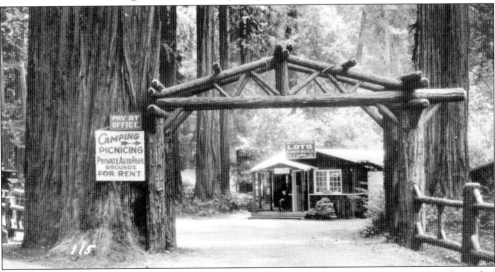

LA HONDA PARK ENTRANCE, 1941. The 1931 sales literature describes what to expect from this park: "La Honda Park, in the midst of miles of giant redwoods, a restful retreat for which you have been looking; not far from home, yet far enough to help you forget the troubles and cares of business. The most beautiful spot in San Mateo County. Pure spring water piped to camps and cabins. Picnicking, boating, camping, swimming. Parking fee 50 cents per car; camp tents $7.00 per week. Cabin lots, creek and woods, $400 up. Bartley & Woodhams. Phone La Honda 5." (Courtesy Rob and Kathy [Zanone] Wolf.)

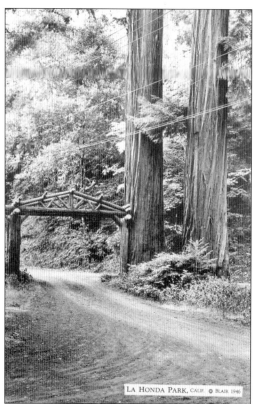

LA HONDA PARK, CALIF. © BLAIR 1946

PARK ENTRANCE, 1947. Here is another view of La Honda Park from the inside looking out. La Honda Park was where a motor home park is now located. La Honda Park had a dance floor and was the favorite meeting place for teenagers during the summers. (Courtesy Charlie Catania.)

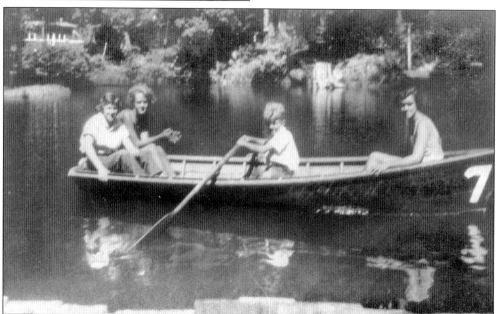

BOATING IN LA HONDA PARK. The creek was dammed each year for swimming and boating. A swollen creek tore out the sides of the dam in the 1940s, and it was never repaired. The rest of the park remained open without the lake. This photograph shows the lake created from the dammed creek. (Courtesy Rob and Kathy [Zanone] Wolf.)

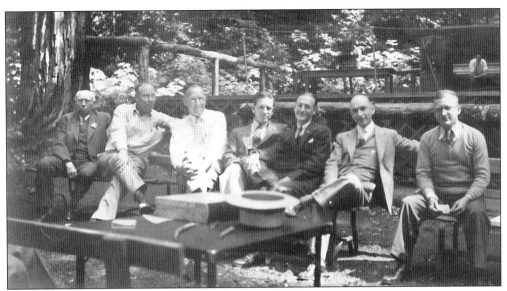

ORIGINAL CUESTA DIRECTORS, C. 1932. Cuesta La Honda Guild is a homeowners' association for about 300 homes in La Honda. The guild provides water, maintains roads, and provides recreation facilities for the community. This photograph is of Jim Allen, one of the guild's founders, with the other directors. A later Cuesta La Honda Guild president of note is Judd Cochran, who helped organize the La Honda Days festivals and planted and maintained a flower garden next to Reflection Lake. The community recognized his contributions in 1990 by creating the Judd Cochran Community Park. (Courtesy Cuesta La Honda Guild.)

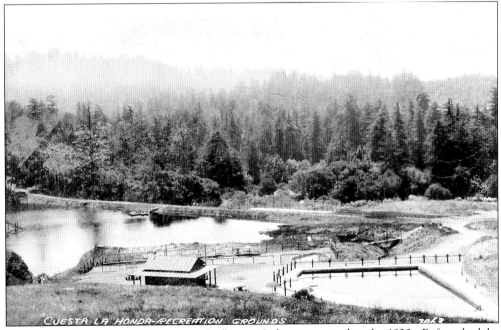

REFLECTION LAKE JUST COMPLETED. Reflection Lake was created in the 1920s. Before the lake was built, a dairy was located at that spot. The road past the lake on the far side serves as a dam. This photograph must have been taken shortly after the lake was created since nothing is growing yet around its perimeter. (Courtesy George and Mary Bordi.)

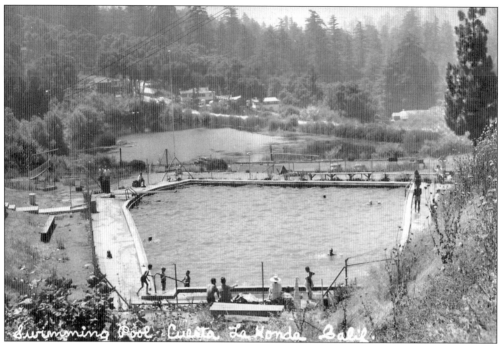

CUESTA SWIMMING AND REFLECTION LAKE. The original Cuesta swimming pool had a view of Reflection Lake and beyond. The pool has since been replaced, and trees have blocked much of the view down toward the lake. Fishing tournaments were held in Reflection Lake in the 1960s and early 1970s. (Courtesy Milton Cavalli.)

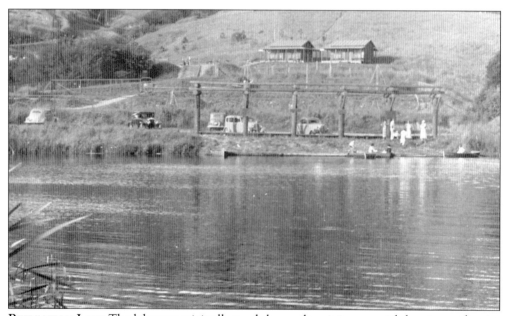

REFLECTION LAKE The lake was originally much larger than it is now, with boating and a pier for fishing. For a while in the 1970s, swans lived there but were mysteriously missing one day. A plaque honoring one of the swans, Princess, is still at the lake. The mens' and womens' bathhouses can be seen in the background. (Courtesy Charlie Catania.)

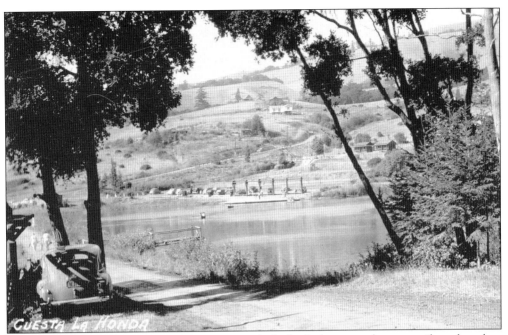

REFLECTION LAKE. The lake is a migratory path for birds, but over the years, silt and neglect have hurt the lake's health. There are also rumors that cars were driven into the lake and left there, but that has not been confirmed. (Courtesy Milton Cavalli.)

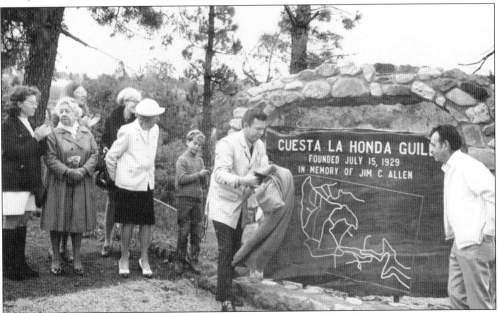

DEDICATION TO JIM ALLEN. A memorial plaque was erected by the guild for Jim Allen, who took care of Cuesta La Honda in the early 1930s. The plaque can still be seen across the road from Reflection Lake. Allen was also the person who removed Carter's Stump and exclaimed at the time, "We ruined saw after saw on that old stump. It was full of bullets. Just full of bullets. Finally we just sawed it off at ground level and let it be part of the road." (Courtesy Cuesta La Honda Guild.)

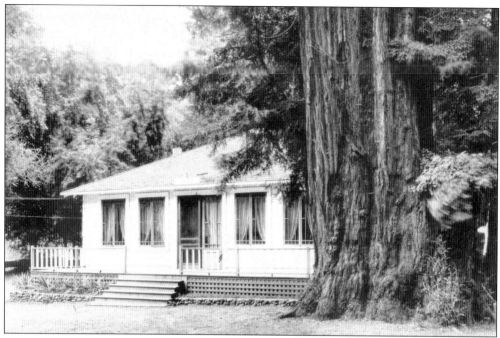

TROUTMERE OR BIG TREE INN. Both Troutmere and Big Tree have been used as a name for the inn here. Troutmere Fish Farm has been a fixture in La Honda since about 1905. Troutmere is located a couple miles west of La Honda and was originally used as a holding pond for redwood logs. A Troutmere lamppost and some windows had come from the 1915 Panama Pacific International Exposition in San Francisco (Courtesy Charlie Catania.)

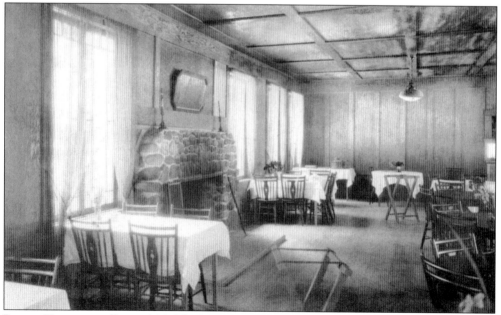

INSIDE TROUTMERE INN, 1926. This is a view inside the dining room of Troutmere Inn. The table in back has a Victrola record player on it. Of course, fresh trout was on the menu from the nearby Troutmere fish farm. (Courtesy Karen Delee.)

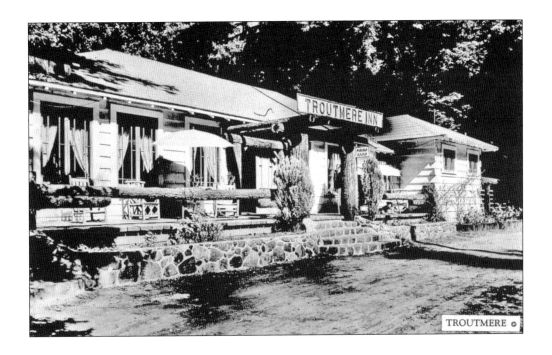

ORIGINAL TROUTMERE INN. Dr. R. W. Krobitzsch created Troutmere Fish Farm and Troutmere Guernsey Farm and developed the Redwood Terrace community across the road from Troutmere. Dr. Krobitzsch was also a merchant of exotic feathers. He traveled the world to acquire his merchandise for the fashion industry in the 1920s. Below is a more current view of the inn. (Above courtesy Rick and Kit Paden; below courtesy Charlie Catania.)

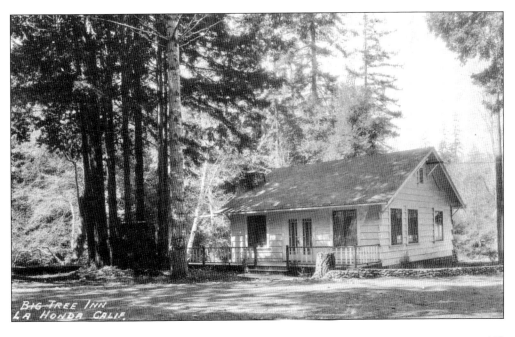

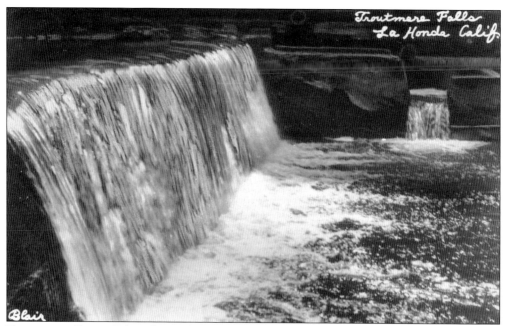

TROUTMERE FALLS. When the creek was allowed to be diverted through the hatchery, it created a spectacular falls. Water now must be pumped to create the waterfall. (Courtesy Rob and Kathy [Zanone] Wolf.)

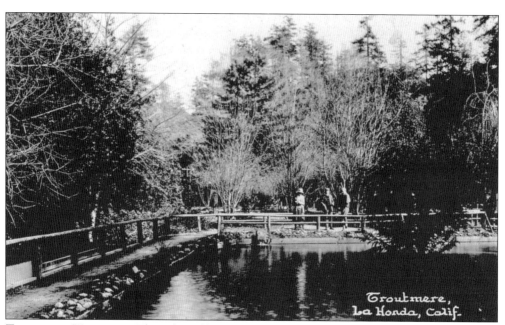

TROUTMERE HATCHERY. The pole and bait are free there, and the fish are priced by size. The inn is now gone, but Troutmere is still open for fishing on weekends during the summer. (Courtesy Kit and Rick Paden.)

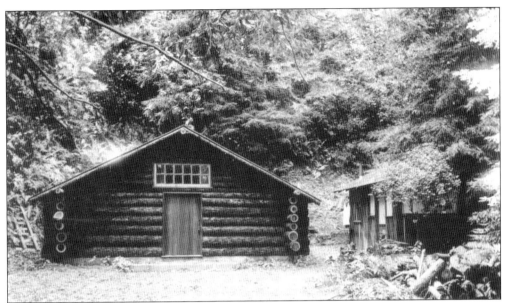

CABIN NEAR TROUTMERE. This log cabin was located near the Troutmere property. (Courtesy Rob and Kathy [Zanone] Wolf.)

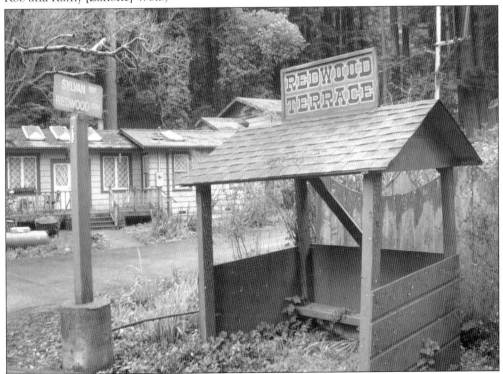

REDWOOD TERRACE AREA. Dr. R. W. Krobitzsch, who owned Troutmere, developed Redwood Terrace as a summer retreat area. During Prohibition, there was a still at the top of Redwood Terrace. Dr. Mize was said to have run a speakeasy there. Some of the houses were wired to the speakeasy with a system of buzzers that may have been used as an alert system if the police were coming up the hill. There have been reports of ghosts around the speakeasy area. (Courtesy author.)

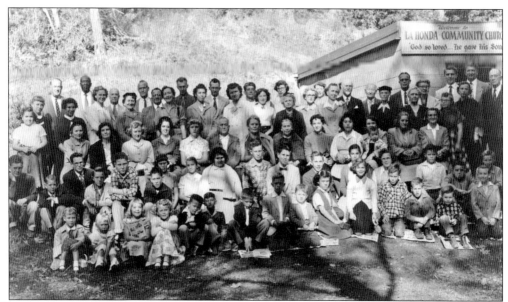

SAM MCDONALD. Emanuel "Sam" McDonald was a descendent of slaves and started working for Stanford University in 1903. He worked there for 50 years, eventually becoming superintendent of athletic grounds and buildings. When he died in 1957, he left his 400-plus acres of La Honda redwood forest to Stanford to use as a park. The land was sold to San Mateo County and is now part of Sam McDonald Park. This photograph shows Sam McDonald at the La Honda Community Church. He is located in the back row, second from the left. (Courtesy Pam McReynolds.)

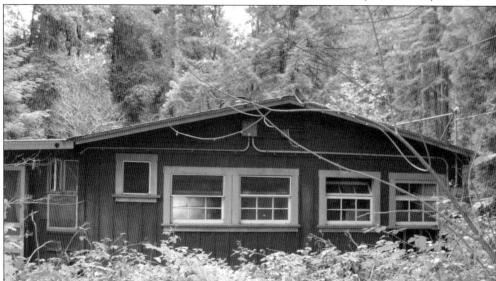

SAM MCDONALD'S CABIN. Sam McDonald called his lodge Chee-Chee-Wa-Wa. Sam McDonald reminisced about his home in his memoirs, *Sam McDonald's Farm*, writing "I have journeyed there after my day's work that I might rest and work and meditate and pray in the seclusion of nature's sanctuary." Sam McDonald goes on to mention the "co-operation and true friendship of my La Honda neighbors," including James Burn, Pete Towne, the Bartleys, the Woodhamses, Matt Grant, the Searses, Cavallis, Allens, Callans, Boones, Lehners, Alsfords, McMillans, and Mrs. Archie Widemeyer. (Courtesy author.)

Eight

PARTIES AND PRANKSTERS

Searsville, over the hill near Woodside, was known as a party town, but the town died after the lumber ran out, and the area was turned into a reservoir around 1891. John Sears, who the town was named after, moved to La Honda. Perhaps Searsville's party reputation followed Sears because La Honda soon acquired a similar reputation. In 1881, the town had both a saloon and a dance hall, and by the early 1900s, there were four hotels and seven saloons around town.

The town celebrated La Honda Bandit Days and rodeos in the 1940s and 1950s. In 1950, Jack Glass, Cy Williams, Basil Willett, and other community members formed the La Honda Canyon Community Hall Society, which sponsored the first junior rodeo in 1954 to raise funds for the local fire department. In 1967, the town celebrated the first La Honda Days, which included the strangely named First 88th Annual International Banana Slug Racing Championships. The origin of this race was a dubious story about how the Younger brothers, taking a saloon break while building the store, made a bet of how long it would take a slug to reach the end of the bar. A 1967 newspaper described the two-day La Honda Days events as follows: "Log rolling, slug racing, raffles, displays and a firemans' ball . . . Four local bands will perform. . . . The crowning of Miss La Honda Days will follow." The parade went down Highway 84 from the fire station to where Boots and Saddle was located.

Many interesting characters lived in town over these years, including a woman named Harrit Bowan, who flew her airplane into the Redwood Terrace area of La Honda in the 1940s and never left. Her plane was in her yard and was partially dismantled in her house, and she was often seen riding her bike to Half Moon Bay, usually to get chips, sodas, and cigarettes. The locals called her—and some may have even believed her to be—Amelia Earhart.

By 1969, the place was overrun by people from over the hill. The 1971 La Honda Days had a miniature merry-go-round and a Ferris wheel next to the firehouse. Sunday was to be parade day, but that day turned ugly. A motorcyclist knocked down a woman with a chain and then ran over her head outside of Venturi's bar; she never recovered. Vandalism was rampant, and seven sheriff cars were called. That was the last year of La Honda Days.

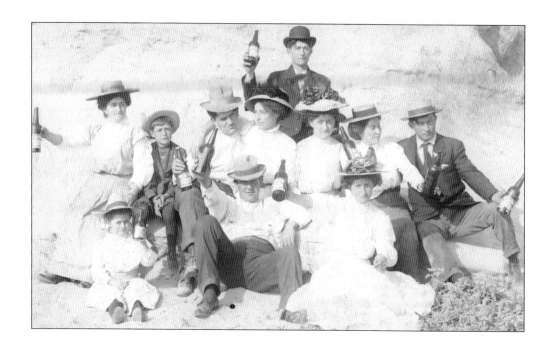

BEACH OUTING. These photographs shows San Gregorio beach outings for La Honda locals. Pictured in the above photograph are the following: (first row, from left to right) Amelia Bonturi, Matt Zanoni, and Virginia Silva; (second row) Cary Berta, Bob Zanoni, Louie Zanoni, Anne Forni, Emma Pera, unidentified, Plenio Zanoni; (third row) Henry Zanoni. (Above courtesy Milton Cavalli; below courtesy Rob and Kathy [Zanone] Wolf.)

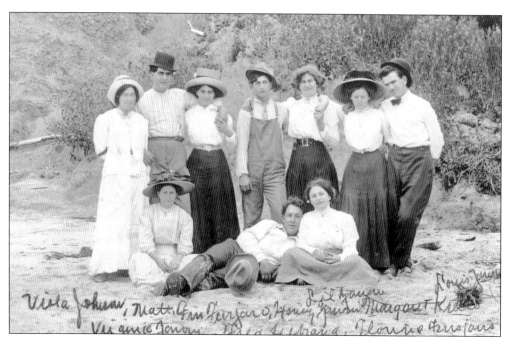

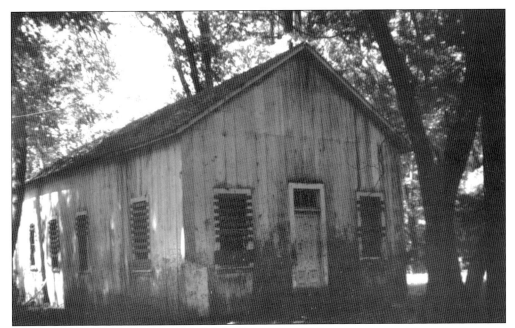

SEARS DANCE HALL. On July 4, 1877, John Sears's son, William, announced from the Sausman Store in Old La Honda that his father and he were going to build a store, hotel, dance hall, and barn three-fourths of a mile east, near the old bear pit. In 1881, they kept their promise, and also built a saloon, stable, and blacksmith shop. The photograph shows the Sears dance hall in 1940. (Courtesy Bud Foss.)

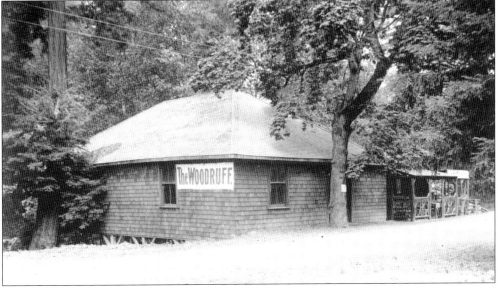

WOODRUFF DANCE HALL, 1924. This dance hall was located adjacent to the Woodruff Inn, and was still operating after the Woodruff Inn burned down in 1923. Another dance hall, owned by Edgar Woodhams and Edgar Bartley, was called Woodhams dance hall. It was located across the street from Applejack's saloon. During the 1920s, dances were held there every Saturday night. The hall was lit by kerosene lamps, and Pete Towne played the piano, or bands would come in from Half Moon Bay. (Courtesy Pam McReynolds.)

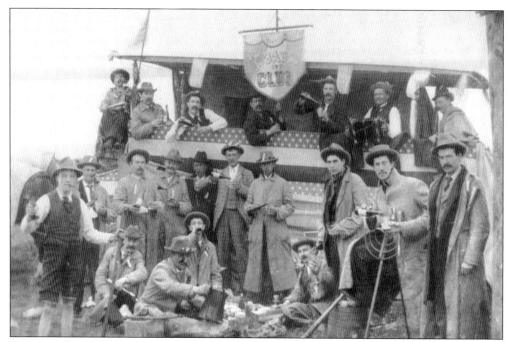

Tobacco Club Outing in La Honda. This appears to be an interesting group, which seems to be associated by a common bond of cigars, alcohol, and accordion music. The only note on the back of this photograph is that "Uncle Will" Horabin is in the wagon under the small flag. (Courtesy Redwood City Library.)

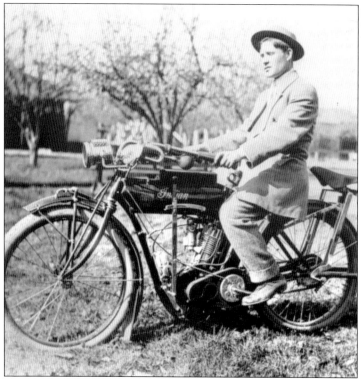

Early Motorcyclist, c. 1910. Perhaps this trendsetter started the current tradition of motorcyclists descending upon La Honda on warm summer weekends. The photograph of this early biker was taken at the Weeks ranch. The motorcycle was made by the Indian Company. (Courtesy Redwood City Library.)

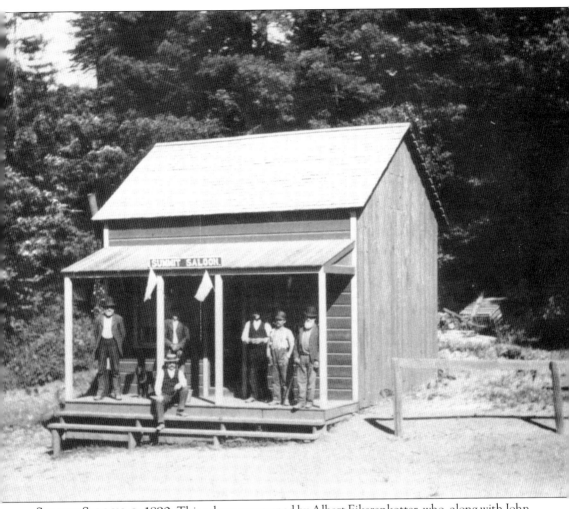

SUMMIT SALOON, C. 1890. This saloon was owned by Albert Eikerenkotter, who, along with John Sears, was a founder of Searsville. The saloon was located on Old La Honda Road near Skyline Boulevard. Jesse Rapley opened a roadhouse just across the road from this saloon. Eikerenkotter married Rapley's daughter Minnie. (Courtesy Charlie Catania.)

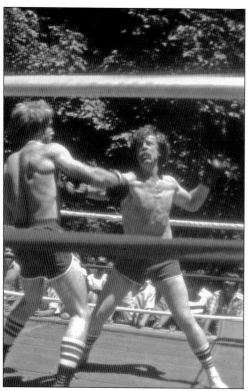

BOXING AT BOOTS, 1978. Hundreds of spectators showed up for a boxing match between Pat Williams and Jim Conn at Boots and Saddles on July 4, 1978. What began as a personal difference between two local residents ended as an event. John Lindstrom built the stage, and the ropes came from Log Cabin Ranch. There were so many bets on the fight that the rumor was that the outcome was only called a draw to prevent more fights. The boxing stage was left there and was used later for other events, including weddings. (Courtesy Pat Williams, Carol Williams, and David Strohm.)

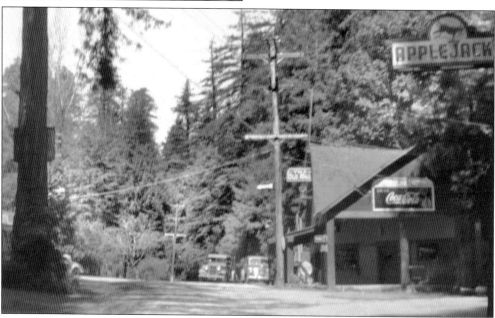

APPLEJACK'S SALOON, C. 1940. Applejack's, a registered California landmark, was originally a blacksmith shop built in 1879 by John Sears. Applejack kept local animals, such as raccoons and bobcats, in cages alongside the building to show tourists. Once an old-timers' bar, it is now the center of activity on weekends. The neon Applejack's sign shown in this 1940 photograph looks much the same today. (Courtesy Bud Foss.)

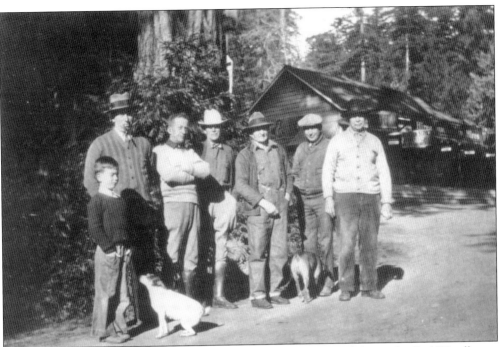

APPLEJACK GABRIELLE, PROPRIETOR. The photograph shows, from left to right, Bud Woodhams, Frank Cavalli, John "Applejack" Gabrielle, unidentified, Jack Wilson, unidentified, and John Young. Applejack owned Applejack's saloon and an apple orchard just west of town. (Courtesy Rob and Kathy [Zanone] Wolf.)

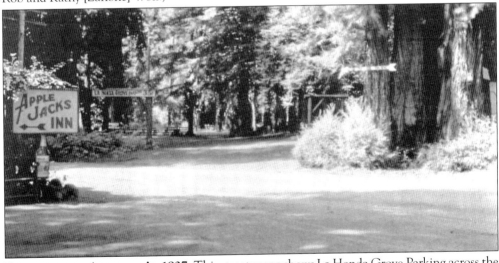

PARKING NEAR APPLEJACK'S, 1937. This street scene shows La Honda Grove Parking across the street from Applejack's saloon. Around 1970, Charles Jones, in the book *A Separate Place*, describes Applejack's when it was considered an old-timers' bar as follows: "At times you will find the bar full and fiercely quiet. It is a numbing site to see a dozen or so people draped over drinks in silent meditation of their own dazed stares in the back-bar mirror. Is there a slight gas leak somewhere, just barely stunning the patrons? Are they all philosophers? No. They will shake themselves, or someone coming in will bring a louder mood with him, and the bar will be full and raucous and young again." (Courtesy Rob and Kathy [Zanone] Wolf.)

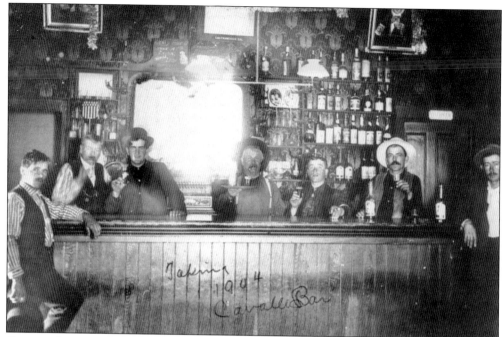

CAVALLI STORE AND BAR, 1904. An old newspaper article states, "On one side was general merchandise, with everything from barrels of pickles to boots, shoes and canned goods. Alcoholic beverages were sold on the other side. Hard boiled eggs were free. A shot of whiskey or glass of steam beer could be gotten for a nickel. The store also housed the village post office and switch board." Patrons in the photograph are (from left to right) Frank Basano, unidentified, Matt Zanoni, James Zanoni, Plenio Zanoni, Manual Santos, and unidentified. (Courtesy Rob and Kathy [Zanone] Wolf.)

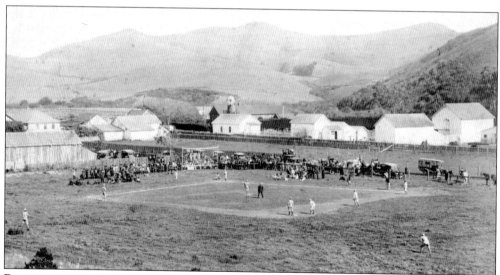

BASEBALL, 1914. By the 1870s, baseball was the favorite team sport in America, and La Honda was no exception. This 1914 game was between the La Honda Monsters and the San Gregorio White Hosiery. (Courtesy Rob and Kathy [Zanone] Wolf.)

BANDIT DAY FIRST PROGRAM, 1948.
Bandit Day began in 1948 and lasted
into the 1950s. According to the
1949 Bandit Day program, the name
"Bandit Day" was chosen for an annual
La Honda celebration because of "the
early history of this beautiful Canyon,
its being a hideout for a good number
of the famous outlaws of the early
west." (Courtesy Hayden Coggins.)

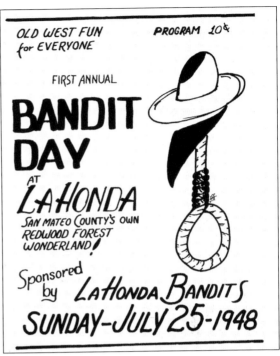

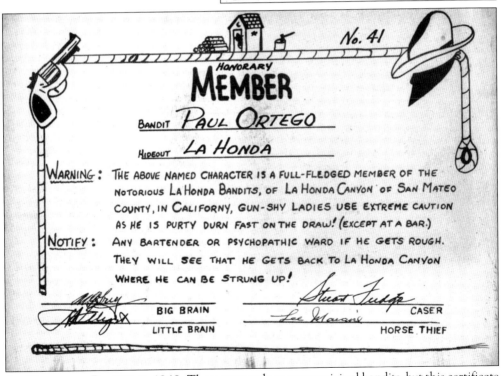

AN HONORARY BANDIT, C. 1948. There were only so many original bandits, but this certificate
epitomizes the fun that the town had back in the late 1940s and 1950s during their Bandit Day
celebrations. The fun was for a good cause, since it raised money for the volunteer fire brigade.
(Courtesy Hayden Coggins.)

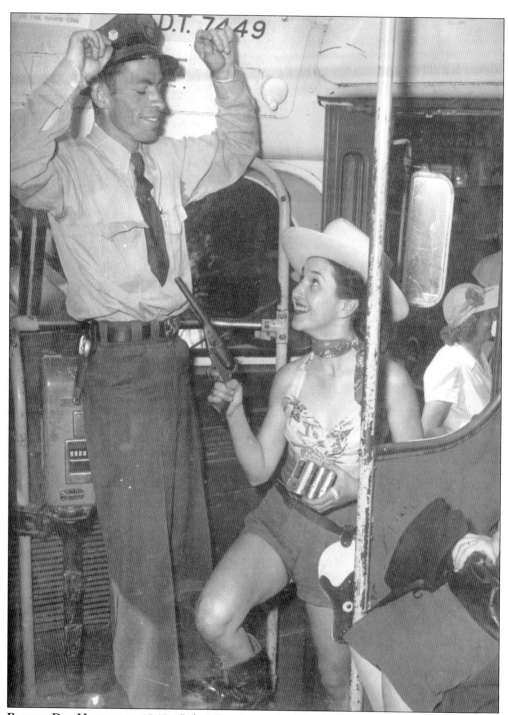

BANDIT DAY HOLDUP, C. 1948. "Babe" Coggins, wife of Hayden Coggins (one of the organizers of the event), holds up a bus driver who brought visitors to the La Honda Bandit Days. This was a promotional shot that captures the spirit of the event. The event officers this year were Bill Grey ("Big Brain"), Russ Elliget ("Little Brain"), Stu Fudge ("Caesar"), and Lee Macaire ("Horse Thief"). (Courtesy Hayden Coggins.)

BABE COGGINS AND RUSS ELLIGET,
c. 1948. This is another Bandit Day
promotional shot with Babe Coggins
and "Sheriff" Russ Elliget, who
ran the mercantile store in town.
(Courtesy Hayden Coggins.)

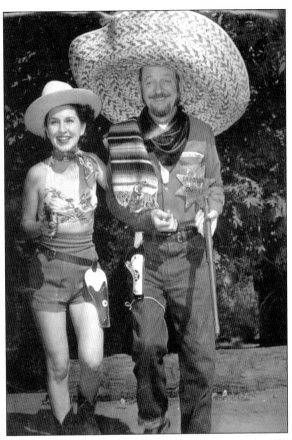

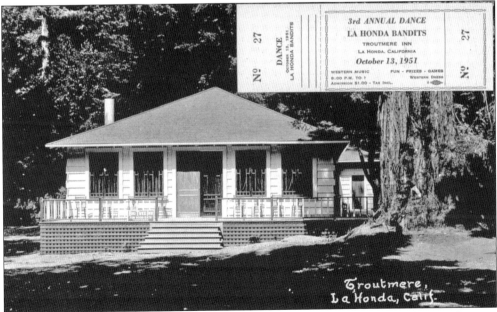

DANCING AT TROUTMERE, 1951. The photograph shows a ticket to a 1951 Bandit Days dance at
the Troutmere Inn. (Courtesy Kit and Rick Paden; inset courtesy Hayden Coggins.)

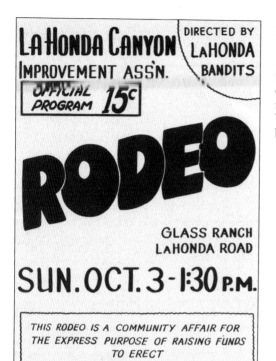

RODEO PROGRAM, C. 1950. The full lineup of events included bronco riding, team roping, steer riding, open stock horse, junior gulf riding (for boys under age 14), calf roping, wild-cow milking, and a baton relay race. These were the days of the movie Westerns, and the rodeos always attracted big crowds. (Courtesy Hayden Coggins.)

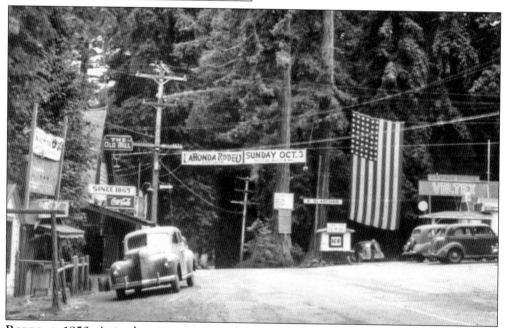

RODEO, C. 1950. A sign hung across town advertising the La Honda Rodeo in 1950, but rodeos had occurred at least as far back as the early 1920s. This rodeo was held at Glass Ranch, which was a couple miles east on La Honda Road where the Red Barn now stands on Midpeninsula Regional Open Space District property. (Courtesy Rob and Kathy [Zanone] Wolf.)

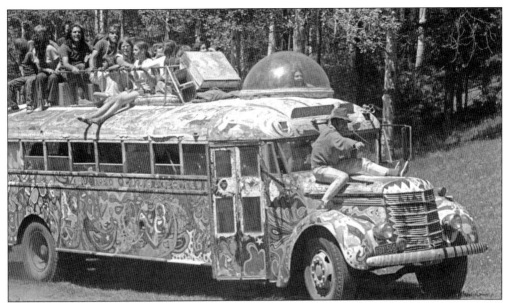

KESEY'S BUS FURTHUR. In 1964, Ken Kesey and his Merry Pranksters wildly painted a 1939 International bus named "Furthur" and drove it around the country to celebrate the publication of Kesey's second book, *Sometimes a Great Notion*. Furthur was created from the words "farther" and "future." Their LSD-fueled multimedia sound-and-light parties were immortalized in Tom Wolfe's book *The Electric Kool-Aid Acid Test*. In 1965, Kesey joined the La Honda Days parade in the Furthur bus. In this photograph taken at the 1968 Great Bus Race in New Mexico, Kesey leads the way from the hood of Furthur. (Copyright © Lisa Law.)

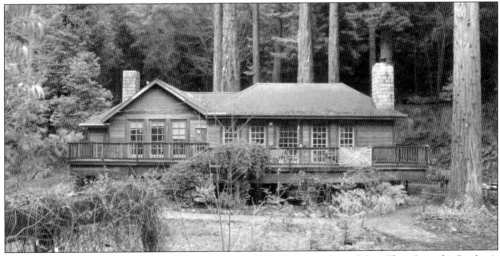

HOME OF KESEY AND THE MERRY PRANKSTERS. Ken Kesey, author of *One Flew Over the Cuckoo's Nest*, and his Merry Pranksters moved into this log cabin just outside town in 1962. His transient residents included Neal Cassady, who was the inspiration for Jack Kerouac's novel *On the Road*; The Warlocks, who became the Grateful Dead; Hells Angels; and Gonzo journalist Hunter S. Thompson. Thompson described Kesey's home in La Honda as "the world capital of madness. There were no rules, fear was unknown, and sleep was out of the question." Kesey eventually went to jail for marijuana possession and was forbidden from returning to La Honda by the terms of his probation in 1967. (Courtesy author.)

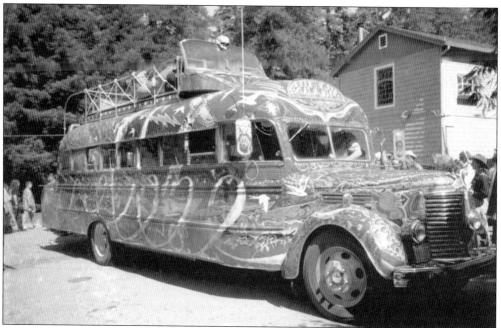

KESEY RETURNS HOME. In 1999, Ken Kesey and the Pranksters returned to La Honda in Furthur II with a British television crew. The reunion and autograph-signing party began at the Merry Prankster Café in town and then moved to Kesey's old cabin, the birthplace of the psychedelic movement. The flood of 1998 destroyed the house, but owners Terry and Eva Adams have restored it back to museum quality. This was to be Ken Kesey's last trip to La Honda; he died two years later. (Courtesy Charlie Catania.)

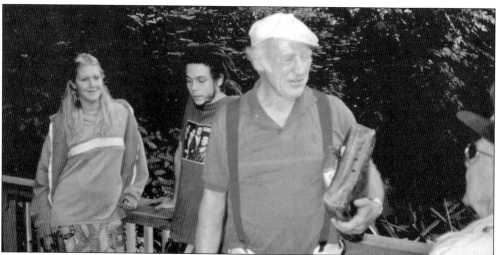

KESEY READS THE *I CHING*. When Ken Kesey returned to his old cabin, he brought everyone into the redwood fairy ring behind the kitchen and held a communal *I Ching* reading. The *I Ching* is an ancient Chinese book of divination. Both of the resulting readings seemed strangely apropos for cabin owner Terry Adams, considering that flooding the previous year destroyed the cabin. One reading said, "A good man confronted with a trial by water will prevail if he is true to himself." Kesey is seen here holding the *I Ching* just after the reading. (Courtesy Terry and Eva Adams.)

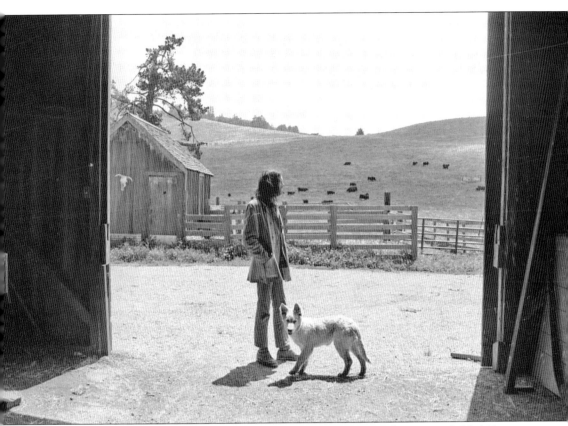

NEIL YOUNG'S BROKEN ARROW RANCH. In the hills near La Honda is a ranch Neil Young purchased in 1970. He has recorded several albums at the Broken Arrow studio there. Graham Nash once told a story about the ranch: "I once went down to Neil's ranch and he rowed me out into the middle of the lake—putting my life in his hands once again. He waved at someone invisible, and music started to play in the countryside. I realized Neil had his house wired as the left speaker and his barn wired as the right speaker. And Elliot Mazer, his engineer, said 'How is it?' And Neil shouted back, 'More barn.'" Neil Young used to come to Venturis Saloon and Boots and Saddles Lodge, where he sometimes played unannounced. Pegi and Neil Young support local artisans, organize the annual concert for the Bridge School, and have provided tremendous support to the community over the years. (Courtesy Henry Diltz.)

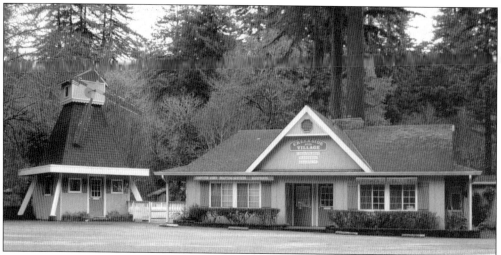

RETROSPECTIVE: THE TOWN. La Honda has had a long reputation as a party town. This photograph shows what used to be a saloon/hotel combination called Venturis in the 1970s. It was a rock-and-roll bar and the most likely place in town to find fights and drugs. Some of the townsfolk still recall the late 1960s and 1970s as a dark time because of these problems. The building now houses businesses with no indication of its wilder past. The windmill is the only reminder of Tom Hoogstraten, the Dutchman who used to own the bar. (Courtesy author.)

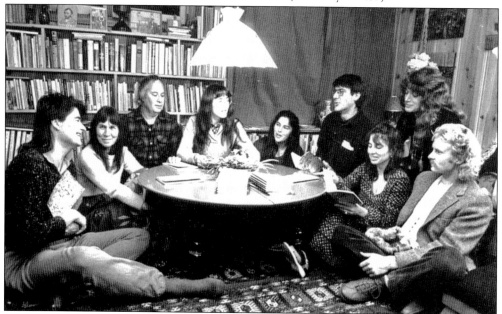

RETROSPECTIVE: THE PEOPLE. La Honda was once home to loggers, ranchers, and farmers, with an influx of campers and hunters during the summers. La Honda is now a bedroom community, and the residents are an eclectic mix of not only artisans, construction workers, and aging hippies, but also engineers, professors, and others looking for a retreat from the hectic pace "over the hill" in Silicon Valley. The town has seen its share of colorful characters over the years who have shaped the unique texture that La Honda has today. This photograph shows the La Honda Poets and Writers Group, which has been an active part of the community since 1980. (Courtesy Paul Fourt.)

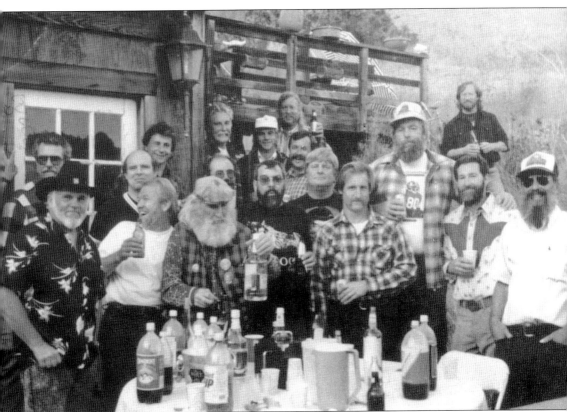

RETROSPECTIVE: THE COMMUNITY. Regardless of their backgrounds and dispositions, the La Honda community is held together by a mutual appreciation of the surrounding natural beauty and history of the area. Continuity of spirit—from the early pioneers, through the Bandit Day festivals of the 1940s, on to today—is maintained through La Honda's annual events: a Cuesta Fourth of July picnic, a country bluegrass festival, a rodeo, and the fire brigade's pancake breakfast and crab cioppino dinner and dance. La Honda is made up of the most wonderful people in the world located in the most beautiful place in the world. This photograph shows a memorial around 1995 for Dan Irhazy, the last owner of Boots and Saddles. (Courtesy Jim Adams.)

BIBLIOGRAPHY

Foss, Werner C. Jr. *History of La Honda*. San Mateo, CA: San Mateo Junior College, June 1941. (Student Monograph available at the San Mateo County History Museum archives.)

Jones, Charles, and photographer Susan Friedman. *A Separate Place*. San Francisco: Sierra Club, 1974.

Margolin, Malcolm. *The Ohlone Way*. Berkeley, CA: Heyday Books, 1978.

Richards, Gilbert. *Crossroads—People and Events of the Redwoods of San Mateo County*. Woodside, CA: Gilbert Richards Publications, 1973.

San Mateo County Historic Resources Advisory Board. *San Mateo County . . . Its History and Heritage*. San Mateo, CA: Self-published by San Mateo County, 1983.

Stanger, Frank M. *Sawmills in the Redwoods: Logging on the San Francisco Peninsula*. San Mateo, CA: San Mateo County Historical Association, 1967.

Stanger, Frank M. *South from San Francisco: San Mateo County, California . . . Its History and Heritage*. San Mateo, CA: San Mateo County Historical Association, 1963.

INDEX

Across America, People are Discovering Something Wonderful. Their Heritage.

Arcadia Publishing is the leading local history publisher in the United States. With more than 3,000 titles in print and hundreds of new titles released every year, Arcadia has extensive specialized experience chronicling the history of communities and celebrating America's hidden stories, bringing to life the people, places, and events from the past. To discover the history of other communities across the nation, please visit:

www.arcadiapublishing.com

Customized search tools allow you to find regional history books about the town where you grew up, the cities where your friends and family live, the town where your parents met, or even that retirement spot you've been dreaming about.

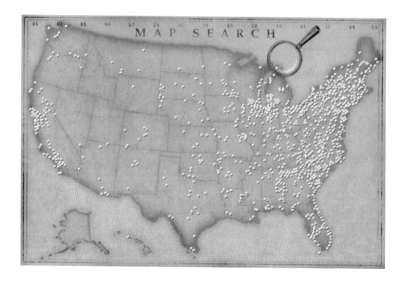